#futureboards

#futureboards

Learn how to create a vision board
to get exactly the life you want

Sarah Centrella

Adams Media

New York   London   Toronto   Sydney   New Delhi

Adams Media
An Imprint of Simon & Schuster, Inc.
57 Littlefield Street
Avon, Massachusetts 02322

First Adams Media hardcover edition July 2019

ADAMS MEDIA and colophon are trademarks of Simon & Schuster.

For information about special discounts for bulk purchases, please contact Simon & Schuster Special Sales at 1-866-506-1949 or business@simonandschuster.com.

The Simon & Schuster Speakers Bureau can bring authors to your live event. For more information or to book an event contact the Simon & Schuster Speakers Bureau at 1-866-248-3049 or visit our website at www.simonspeakers.com.

Interior design by Colleen Cunningham
Interior images © Getty Images/enjoynz, artisteer, _human

Manufactured in the United States of America

10 9 8 7 6 5 4 3 2 1

Library of Congress Cataloging-in-Publication Data
Names: Centrella, Sarah, author.
Title: #FutureBoards / Sarah Centrella.
Description: Avon, Massachusetts: Adams Media, 2019.
Includes index.
Identifiers: LCCN 2019006915 | ISBN 9781507210376 (hc) | ISBN 9781507210383 (ebook)
Subjects: LCSH: Visualization. | Self-realization. | Success.
Classification: LCC BF367 .C46 2019 | DDC 153.3/2--dc23
LC record available at https://lccn.loc.gov/2019006915

ISBN 978-1-5072-1037-6
ISBN 978-1-5072-1038-3 (ebook)

For my babies: Kanen, Mira, and Izzy.

You are the light, love, and joy of my life. You've been my
ever-burning flame, propelling my dreams and creating in me
the relentless pursuit of the woman I am meant to be.
All I do, I do for you.

Dream HUGE, little ones.

Contents

PART ONE: BEFORE 26

Build the Dream Before You Build the Board

Contents

PART TWO: DURING 108

Making Your #FutureBoard

PART THREE: AFTER 154

You've Made Your #FutureBoard, Now What?

Preface

Not to brag or anything, but I have a superpower. It's the uncanny ability to predict my future in near spooky detail with unbelievable accuracy.

I can turn a thought into a real-life *Instagram*-able story. A seemingly impossible dream into a living, breathing, I-can't-believe-this-is-happening selfie. I can take a picture that I found online, put it on my #FutureBoard, and turn it into a once-in-a-lifetime *pinch-me* moment!

Also, here's the thing you should know about me… I like to share. After all, what fun is having a gangsta superpower if you're not willing to share it?

Here are all my manifesting secrets.

Why Should You Listen to Me?

You may be thinking: *Why should I listen to you, Sarah?*

Because a #FutureBoard saved my life.

It was 2009 and I was trying desperately to piece together my life after it imploded the previous year when my husband left our family to pursue his affair. At the time our twin girls were just over a year old and our son was five. We'd been together since our sophomore year of high school, sixteen years, and married for eight. It was inconceivable to be starting my life over with nothing, at age thirty-two. Unthinkable that I'd be a single mother of three babies, trying to survive on my own.

Before he left, we'd filed bankruptcy, lost our home to foreclosure the year our twins were born, *and* it was the recession…the perfect crap storm.

Things were bleak; I was struggling to simply put food on the table, keep the lights on, and pay rent, all while working full-time and learning how to parent alone.

But the benefit of starting from rock bottom is that you've basically been handed a gift: a clean slate. Your pride's been demolished, your ego is pulverized, your fear of failure has been realized in its most brutal forms, you are…free.

Suddenly you're able to shake the judgment of others in a way you never could before, because you no longer give a shit what they think! You've entered a primal survival stage, one you didn't even realize existed. Now all your energy must be reserved for action, for making things happen.

I began to dream.

Though the reality of my daily life was dark and overwhelming, I couldn't help but think: *What if I had a totally different life? What if I could create anything I wanted?* I was no longer tied to someone else's idea of what my future should hold, and that alone began to open my mind to new possibilities. Slowly, I nurtured that tiny seed of hope, which turned into a craving for a better life.

Slowly, I began to *dream*.

I realized that if I wanted to succeed, I'd need to completely reinvent myself and invent an entirely new future for myself and my children. But how? I had no idea and it seemed like an impossible task.

I didn't know much about how to change my life back then, but I did start doing something that would change everything. I began to create an alternate "happy place" universe in my mind. It's not a stretch to say that I invented a fantasy life out of thin air.

In this life I imagined myself as a successful businesswoman working in a career I loved. I visualized what this woman looked like in great detail. She was fit, confident, empowered, and respected, a real boss chick! She drove an expensive car and carried a bag that cost an entire paycheck, not because she was materialistic, but because she deserved and could afford it. It was the reward for all her hard work. And hey, she was successful in this future life, so why not?! But best of all, she traveled with her children regularly, showing them the world. She ran marathons and did yoga. She wrote books and gave talks inspiring people to never quit their dreams. She was everything I wanted to be.

She was everything I wanted to be.

I searched for pictures online that visually represented each of these dreams, created my first real #FutureBoard, and then took it to work. It sat behind my laptop in my tiny windowless cubicle and each time I looked at it, I was magically transported into another world. A world filled with hope, possibility, and joy.

It was this ability to shift my focus from my dark, daily reality to this happy imaginary world that saved me. That first year was so devastating and difficult that dwelling on my current situation at the time would have destroyed me. I credit the Universe with helping me transfer the minimal energy I had into this new mental space.

This book shares my journey as I transformed into the fantasy woman I invented on my first (and subsequent) #FutureBoards. Best of all, it teaches you *how* to create the life you want and *how* to visually represent it on your very own #FutureBoard. I'll share examples of how my board has come to life and stories of real people who've followed this method to manifest their dreams.

Everything you'll read in these pages actually happened. I know they'll seem unbelievable; sometimes I can hardly believe them! I've manifested some insanely cool experiences (and things) the past few years, not the least of which is *you*.

You are now part of my journey, and when you start manifesting your dreams, you'll be part of my dream to help others do what I've done.

Introduction

What exactly is a #FutureBoard? A #FutureBoard is a physical (cork) board, proudly displayed in your home or office, that is covered with beautiful photographs intentionally chosen to visually SHOW your future *dream life*.

I call my boards #FutureBoards rather than "vision boards" because to me, they are more than just a "vision" or a "dream." They are actual visual pictures of what my life will look like in the next three to five years and beyond. They show me what my future looks like before I live it. Like I said, they are my superpower, and now they will be yours too!

This book will lead you through three parts to building your #Future-Board and taking the steps toward the life you've dreamed of. The three parts are:

Part One: The Plan

When you build a house, you need a strong foundation before the walls and roof can go up, right? You'll also need an architect. One who can create a blueprint for your dream home, based on what you want. But what if you don't know what you want?

Part One of this book walks you through the process of discovering what you truly want, removing your blocks to getting it, and helps you let go and dream HUGE! You must complete this work *before* you can begin construction (pun intended) of your board. You need this information as it answers vital questions that will tell you what to build.

But a blueprint has its limits. You look at the drawing and you still can't see, or feel, what it would be like to walk around, or live in, your beautiful new home. That's when you'd hire a designer (me!) to help you see the vision. This is where your dreams come to life in your imagination. (Your future life story.)

You guessed it, in this metaphor you're the architect. I'll teach you everything you need to know, so don't stress! You've got this.

Part Two: The Build

Now that you have your blueprint and know what your dream house will look and feel like, your team can commission a custom-created miniature model of your new home. This model is the first time you've physically and visually seen the dream that previously existed only in your mind and on paper (this is your #FutureBoard).

You are thrilled! Your vision is coming to life; you can see it clearly now! You proudly display the model for all to see. You look at it every day for motivation and inspiration to keep hustling for the day when that dream becomes real life. That's exactly what your new #FutureBoard will be: a visual reminder of what you're building. It allows you to see and feel your future life before it happens.

In Part Two you will learn how to create your board, first online and then in the physical form that you'll proudly display on your wall.

Part Three: Making It a Reality

If you've gone to all this work (and expense) would you stop construction on your *actual* house once you have the mini replica? Hell, no! So why do most people create a "vision board" and call it a day? That's just the start of the construction process!

In the final section of this book you'll learn how to build the life you want, the one that's on your board. This is the piece of the puzzle that most manifesting books avoid, the true HOW. And that's exactly what *#FutureBoards* is all about:

1. How to figure out what you want in your future abundant life.

2. How to create a physical, visual, tangible, mini version of that life.

3. And finally, how to actually *live* that life.

Before You Get Started

Over the past few years, I've spent a lot of time conducting #Future-Board workshops and coaching people how to apply the tools you'll learn in this book to create and manifest the life you want. And during these sessions one thing has become very clear: people process the information you're about to learn very differently based on if they identify themselves as a natural "Dreamer" or as a "Thinker."

Knowing this, I've created some special tips throughout this book that will help you translate what you're learning in a way that best aligns with Dreamers or Thinkers. If you happen to be one of the lucky ones who consider yourself a delightful mix of both, then I'm totally jealous of you! But seriously, these little tips might still be helpful.

You could find that in one exercise you're leaning more toward being a Dreamer, but in the next responding more as a Thinker. If that's the case, the tips will hopefully aid you in removing the various blocks to manifesting as they arise. They will also push you to get the most out of each exercise because what you're really going for here are transformative breakthroughs that will lead to lasting results.

You will notice that in Part One of this book there are more tips for Thinkers than Dreamers. This is because much of the content and homework in this first section comes more naturally to Dreamers, so the majority of tips are to aid Thinkers in connecting with the work to get the most from it. The opposite is true for Part Three, that's the section where Dreamers will need a little extra attention.

The beauty of this method is that it recognizes the strengths of both Dreamers and Thinkers. You *need* both skill sets to effectively create and manifest the life you want. Most people don't know how to add those lacking skills, which results in struggling much longer and harder than needed to get desired results. I believe that truly successful people have a mix of both. They possess the ability to dream big *and* are able to create and execute tangible plans.

As a natural Dreamer myself, I lacked the skill set to take a HUGE dream and turn it into a plan that I could effectively accomplish. That's what this method has taught me—how to behave more like a Thinker so I can effectively accomplish my goals.

Are You a Dreamer?

Dreamers *love* to come up with big visions and grand dreams, but we absolutely suck at execution! In fact, what tends to happen is those dreams soon become overwhelming and before we know it, they've actually demotivated us. We get all excited, seeing the possibilities, but the longer we think about it, the more impossible it begins to seem. We start to think about all the work we have to do, then we look at our own previous track record and ability to do that work, and this is where we hit a wall! We throw our hands up in despair, letting another dream vanish into oblivion.

Here's how to tell if you're a Dreamer:

- Do you often daydream?
- Were you a daydreamer as a child?
- Do you consider yourself artistic?

- Do you "see" things in your mind in a vivid or visual way (like a movie in your head)?

- Are you creative?

- Are you a risk taker?

- Does buying a lottery ticket give you secret excitement, a twinge of hope, or even just an excuse to daydream about what you'd do with all that money?

- Have you had a difficult time finding the "right" career path? Or finding your "passion," because so many things interest you at first glance?

- Does it excite you to try new things or visit new places?

- Do you often think that there "must be more to life"?

- Do you get excited about new "big ideas"?

- Did you always feel, deep down, that you were "meant for something more"?

If you answered yes to most of these, then you're what I'd consider a natural Dreamer. You love the "big picture." You can easily visualize and get excited by the best-case scenario of a big vision. You're likely spontaneous, sometimes acting before fully vetting an idea. You need the most help learning how to do the tangible stuff, breaking your dream into smaller, manageable pieces. You struggle to *stay* inspired long enough to start seeing results.

If this is you, keep an eye out for tips in this book labeled Tips for Dreamers.

Are You a Thinker?

Thinkers are *not* naturally adventurous dreamers! You tend to analyze an idea, create a spreadsheet, and then create another one. You are Googlers! You'll research an idea until you've convinced yourself it's the worst plan in the world and then you'll wind up doing nothing. You really struggle seeing the "big picture" because you've researched every possible way your idea could fail. You focus on the details, and if those seem impossible or unlikely, then you really can't see the point in a bigger vision. Sound familiar?

Here's how to tell if you're a Thinker:

- Do you like to make a plan before taking action?
- Do you thrive on structure?
- Do you tend to vet all possible outcomes before making a "risky" move (or most decisions)?
- Are you, generally speaking, pretty organized?
- Do you tend to research, and then research some more?
- Have you stayed in the same career for several years?
- Do you only make goals you know can be accomplished?
- Do you have a hard time getting excited or taking action on something that is outside your comfort zone?
- Do you think buying a lottery ticket is a waste of money?
- Do people in your life who "dream big" scare you a bit or make you anxious?

- Do you tend to make lists, spreadsheets, plans?

- Is your schedule fairly predictable?

- Does trying new things and going new places scare you or give you anxiety?

- Does failure scare you?

- Are you budget conscious?

If you've been nodding your head as you read most of these questions, then you're what I would consider a Thinker, someone who is naturally more analytical. Even if only 60 percent of those questions apply to you, you're probably more of a Thinker than a Dreamer. I know this, because I could answer *No* to all those! Even ones where I wish my answer was *Yes*.

As a Thinker, you're likely more analytical than impulsive, more structured than spontaneous. I'm guessing you dig facts and logic. You also might frequently second-guess yourself, talking yourself out of taking action.

So dreaming big and visualizing will be tough for you. But the good news is, you'll learn all the skills you need to move past these blocks. If this is you, keep an eye out for tips labeled Tips for Thinkers.

homework

We need to make a pact. You ready? I pledge to tell you everything I know about how to create and manifest the life you want. That's my promise. Now I need you to promise to DO EVERY SINGLE HOME-WORK ASSIGNMENT. If you don't, this book will be a waste of your time. If you do, it will change your life.

I also need you to show up to this process with fresh eyes and an open heart. If you do, I'll lead you right through the homework and exercises that I use with my personal clients and you *will* get results.

With that in mind, here is your first homework assignment: I believe it's important for you to write down (yes, I want you to grab a journal and a pen and *write* old-school style) where you are today as you begin this journey. Be completely honest with yourself; don't hold anything back.

Write the truth. Be brave.

Believe it or not, this is the start of your personal success story. This will soon become your "before." That's why it's so important to get *real* with yourself. You can't change what you haven't identified, so put it all on paper. No one's going to judge you. No one besides you ever even needs to read it. But you've got to do it. Because as you start to see results, you'll soon forget what it felt like when you started. This will help remind you of how far you've come.

Answer these questions in your journal and include today's date:

- What does your life look like right now, today? Describe it. Where do you work? Do you like your job? Where do you live? Do you like your home? Who lives with you? How do you feel about the people in your life?

- What do you wish you could change in your life? Examples: money, physical appearance, the people, your job.

- What is the main thing that is not working in your life today?

- Who is in your life? Who are your friends? Who do you most talk to? Is there anything about this you'd change?

- What's your financial situation like? What would you change?

- How do you physically feel? Are you as healthy and fit as you want to be? Do you have energy? How's your diet?

- How do you mentally feel? Are you sad? Depressed? Happy? How do you currently protect and recharge your mind? What are your most common thoughts about?

What I love about journal writing is that sometimes things pour out of you that you never expected. Let the truth bubble up, because when it does, you then have a starting point for change.

Sometimes all you need is to see it in black and white. This knowledge can set you free. It can put you on a path to defining what you want and getting the tools and support to make the changes you desire a reality.

Good job! I'm proud of you for taking action; you've just completed your first step!

Build the Dream Before You Build the Board

Before you can make your physical #FutureBoard you must first do the foundational work necessary to effectively create your future life. This process is a critical part of creating a board that will actually *work*, one that reflects your dreams and vision for the life you're creating. It's intended to uncover what's been holding you back and to provide tools and homework to aid you in removing blocks to manifesting.

You'll learn how to recognize and control what's going on in your mind so your thoughts are aligned with manifesting your desired outcomes. You'll discover one of my big secrets: how to begin living the life you want *now* (before you're rich!). Also, you'll learn to push your imagination to dream HUGE, focusing on *experiences* over *things*—this shift will blow your mind and open up a world of new possibilities! I'll also introduce you to former clients and people from around the world who've been following my manifesting method to incredible (and life-changing) results.

But the most important piece of this part is discovering what you *actually want* in all areas of your life. I'll walk you through how to answer that million-dollar question so you'll be prepared to find the photos for your board in Part Two.

Reminder: As always, the homework in each section is the only way you can translate what you're learning into your personal life. It is the *only* way to get results. So please, for the love of all things good, do the homework!

01: THE POWER OF "WHAT IF?"

This little chapter sets the framework for *everything*. Learning to shift your perspective on these two simple words (*what if?*) will begin your transformation. I want to turn traditional thinking on its head, giving you the permission and tools to completely reimagine your life. Approach the material in this chapter with an open, receptive mind and allow it to penetrate all the doubtful crevasses of your subconscious, and in doing so, the work has begun!

Embracing Your "What If?"

What if your life was different? What if everything you wrote in that last assignment was *not* your reality? What if you had the power to make it different? *Would you?*

Of course you would! You already *are*. Your present reality is simply a temporary state.

You probably knew this already, but just in case...you *do* have the power to make your life anything you want it to be. You just might need a little help (as we all do sometimes) knowing *what to do* and *how to do it*. And for that, you've got me!

One of the first lessons I learned when I started rebuilding my life was to give hope a fighting chance. When I think back to the days after my ex-husband left, I thank my lucky stars that I gave "what if" and the hope it represented room to breathe. In the midst of my darkest hour, when all logical options seemed impossible, when it felt like there was no way on earth I could survive with my children on my own, hope said, "But, what if you *can*?"

That little thought was the origin of everything.

And today, I'm asking the same of you. I want *you* to give hope room to breathe. Don't squash it. Give it time to work its magic on your thoughts, your beliefs, and your life.

What if your life was everything you ever dreamed it could be? *What if* you had wealth and abundance and never worried about money? *What if* you had a body you loved and felt fit and healthy? *What if* you had relationships filled with joy, mutual respect, and happiness? *What if* you had a job you loved? *What if* you traveled the world? *What if* you were the person you dream you could be, living the life you dream of living?

What then? Who would you be? What would that life look like? That is the million-dollar question!

This is going to be especially tough for you Thinkers out there, because the idea of "what if" is not a "logical" one. It requires you to step out of your comfort zone and allow thoughts to mill around in your brain that are normally terminated upon inception!

I need you to get out of your head about this. Don't make it more than it is. Keep it simple.

I know your brain is probably saying "This is a waste of time!" Or, "This doesn't make sense, why bother?" I get it.

I need you to counter that argument with: "Sarah told me to do this, so I'm just doing it because she said I had to." That will be a great start! Sometimes thinking of it as something I've told you to do, rather than something you're trying to "buy into," can help alleviate some of that resistance.

homework

What are some positive "what ifs" that you'd like manifested in your new life? Grab your journal and write down at least fifteen. Start each sentence with "What if I..." Try to take a moment with each one and start to imagine that "what if" being your reality. What would it feel like? What would it be like?

Pro tip: If you're struggling here, an easy way to make a list of positive "what ifs" is to think of everything you'd normally see in a negative light. For example: If you'd previously say: "I can't start that business, because *what if* it fails?" Switch it to: "*What if* the business I dream of starting is a *huge* success?" Honestly, that's a far more interesting and relevant question. Think about it—what if that business is a bigger success than you can imagine from where you sit today? Then what? What the heck would you do? Do you have a plan for that? What would your growth strategy be? How much revenue would the business make at its optimum level of performance? How many employees would you hire? What would your office look like? Would you eventually sell it for a huge profit or pass it on to your children? See how many important, burning questions are waiting for your direction and answers? That business can't succeed as long as you're asking only the one dooming question: "What if it fails?"

With each item on your list, see how many follow-up questions you can ask to unpack what you'll do when that positive "what if" manifests (the way I've done in the previous example).

Now let the items on your list mentally marinate! Don't analyze them. Don't question them. Don't start freaking out about *how* you are going to make them happen. Just let them breathe! Reread your list often, keep it fresh in your mind. Allow daydreaming to begin... *What if...you were in Paris right now...ahhh!*

REAL-LIFE SUCCESS STORY

Linzi Boswell
SCOTLAND, UK

"I live in a safe and comfortable home, decorated the way I like."

In the spring of 2017, I received notice from my landlady that she was going to sell the home my daughter and I had lived in for the past seven years. I immediately entered a tailspin of panic, worry, and anxiety. *What were we going to do?* I had followed Sarah on social media for several years and watched her life change, so I decided to take a chance and reach out to her. Sarah personally coached me through her method for manifesting during an extremely difficult time in my life. During this time my daughter and I moved from our home and were squeezing into my father's house, sharing a bedroom. It felt hopeless.

But Sarah reminded me to daily practice what I was learning and recite the motto I'd written: *"I live in a safe and comfortable home, decorated the way I like."* I made my #FutureBoard and included pictures of a cozy home.

At that time rents in our area were out of my price range and purchasing a house seemed out of the question. But then I spoke to a financial adviser and found out I was eligible for home buyer's assistance. I decided to take a leap of faith and view a flat to get a "feel" for what it would be like to walk into my own home. Instantly I felt comfortable and at home in the space. Yikes! This was scary. It was feeling more and more real as I allowed my hopes to grow.

I printed pictures of that exact flat and added them to my #FutureBoard with my motto written around the photos. I remember being scared to even fill out the application for assistance, because what if I was not approved and the dream didn't happen? It felt very scary to allow myself to dream. But Sarah kept pushing me to move past the fear and see that "what if" from a different perspective. "What if you do get it?" she asked me. She reminded me that if I focused on the fear, I would manifest the result of that fear and not the house!

So I filled out the application forms, hoping the flat would still be available if my loans got approved. Waiting was so stressful, and doubts began to creep back in. I knew I needed to focus on the feeling of living in that home, so one day my daughter and I went window-shopping for *our new home*. Taking pictures

of lamps, furniture, and design ideas, allowing ourselves to get excited at the possibility. What if we did get it?! Just the thought was thrilling.

We printed those pictures and added them to our #FutureBoard. Whenever I felt a wobble or doubt threaten to steal my excitement, I looked at those pictures and recited my motto.

My hustle and belief paid off and in mid-December 2017, we received the keys to that very same flat!

When I began working with Sarah it was out of fear and desperation, facing homelessness. I never imagined that six months later I would be a homeowner! Working with Sarah taught me how to believe in myself, my dreams, and the power of the Universe. I'm grateful every day that we now have a lovely home that no one can sell out from under us.

Linzi is a single mom from Scotland. She's now a certified life coach in my coaching program teaching other women how to create and live their dreams the way she has.

Personal Example

In May of 2018 I manifested a two-week trip of a lifetime with my children to London, Ireland, and Scotland and got a chance to personally give Linzi a huge hug! It was a blistery, rain-soaked afternoon in Edinburgh, Scotland. She'd taken the train from her hometown an hour away and my kids were enjoying a little downtime in our city center apartment. We ordered pots of piping hot tea and scones in the little café where J.K. Rowling wrote the first Harry Potter book. It was a magical moment. But that trip was actually the dream of my daughters, Mira and Izzy (age ten). They were the ones who'd put those pictures on their #FutureBoards and for months kept asking when I'd take them to London (Mira's dream destination) and Ireland (Izzy's).

When a #FutureBoard workshop opportunity came up in Scotland, I knew it was the moment we'd been waiting for! Because it was really my girls who manifested the trip, I had them decide where we went! I asked Izzy again if she was sure she wanted to go to Ireland. "Yes!" she said resolutely. "What are we going to do there?" I was curious to know. I didn't know much about Ireland, but a quick *Google* search showed these as the top tourist attractions: green hills, sheep, cows, pubs, Guinness, and whisky! "There might not be much for you to do," I said. She was undeterred.

"Okay," I said. "Here's my laptop, go find pictures of the places you want to go and things you want to do." Thanks to Izzy, we stood above the Cliffs of Moher in a hailstorm, awestruck, looking down at an angry sea. Also because of her, we stayed in a charming cottage in the middle of nowhere, surrounded by sheep and cows for three days. It was pure magic!

But on the day we took a road trip to Galway, I discovered her true fascination with Ireland. Ed Sheeran! It just so happened (I'm sure she planned this perfectly) that the day we visited Galway was the town's annual Ed Sheeran festival. He was playing a sold-out show that night and the entire town was littered with life-sized cutouts and plastered with posters of his face. Smart girl, that one!

Thanks to Mira's online photo dreaming, we stood at the alter in St. George's Chapel at Windsor Castle, ten days before Harry and Meghan exchanged vows in that very spot. My son, Kanen, gets some credit here too. His time online is responsible for the day we spent taking the train to Dover, climbing above the white cliffs and exploring Dover Castle. It's trips like this, moments like these, that I *live* for. Those are memories we will share for the rest of our lives because of the tools you will learn in this book. It's an incredible way to live, believing in the power of our dreams and the possibility of *what if?*

Summary

It's an incredible way to live.

I know this might seem almost too simple to work, but I swear it's magic! "What if" is such a powerful tool; don't underestimate it. From this moment on, your brain will raise a red flag every time you (or anyone else) verbally expresses a negative "what if." It will flash like a giant "Danger!" sign across your mind. When that happens, your job is to set them (or yourself) straight, and reverse the "what if."

02: WHAT'S BLOCKING YOU? CHANGING THE "BROKE" MINDSET

There are three primary blocks to manifesting that I'll tackle in this and the subsequent two chapters. They are:

1. The "broke" mindset.
2. The "I'm not worthy" mindset.
3. The "low-key martyr" mindset.

To date, I've never coached a single person who didn't have one of those three blocks. So my guess is that one or more will reveal itself for you as well. Trust me, I've suffered from all three; I can relate. It's not fun to dig this deep and reveal these hidden beliefs about yourself. It's uncomfortable. It might even be emotional. But you *have* to do it; it's a critical part of this journey.

I'll be honest: these three chapters can be pretty *intense*. A lot will be covered in these chapters, so take it slowly and absorb and apply what you're learning. It is all about recognizing and removing your blocks to manifesting the life you want, which sounds simple, but done right (through giving 100 percent to each homework assignment) it will go deep.

Uncovering and changing thinking patterns and lifelong beliefs is not an easy or comfortable task, but in my coaching experience, this work brings clients some of the most immediate and life-changing results.

This chapter focuses on the "broke" mindset. It's by far the most common block my clients and readers face. Many of its roots are deeply seeded in our subconscious, so even if you don't struggle with money issues, this chapter can still be very eye-opening.

Be patient with yourself and keep pushing for the transformational breakthrough this chapter will uncover. The deeper you take it, the more your life will change. I will walk you through how to transform your mindset and story, remove your excuses, and recognize and change your beliefs about money and about yourself.

There are functional tools in this chapter that should become part of your toolbox moving forward. They are intended to be your "life hacks"—apply them in various situations to retain control of your thoughts, future, and life. I think of them as literal tools, the way a contractor carries a toolbox (hammers, saws, nails, drills, and so on). You will now take these with you to ensure you're prepared for anything. Over time, they will just be how you react to situations and thoughts moving forward. It's time to banish your "lack of money" hang-ups.

Identifying the "Broke" Mindset

The "broke" mindset is simply the belief (conscious or subconscious) that you don't have, and probably will never have, "enough money." That getting money is *hard*.

Blocks to manifesting like this one can be one of the most frustrating and annoying parts of the manifesting process because they're often subconscious, long-held beliefs. Through my years of coaching, I've learned how to spot blocks pretty quickly in clients, but I've also learned that identifying them in your own life is much more difficult. *Why?* Because your blocks are often so deeply embedded in your subconscious that you don't even realize they're there. You might be doing all the right things on a conscious level like *saying* you want something, but all the while your subconscious beliefs are producing the opposite outcome.

For example: If you were raised without much money, in a home where your parents believed (and drilled into you) that money (or lack of) was the reason life was so hard, then it's probably difficult for you to have a positive relationship with money as an adult. If, as a child, you heard them say things like: *money doesn't grow on trees, you have to work hard just to get by, we don't have money for that, rich people are bad,* or anything similar, those become your underlying beliefs about money.

Here's the frustrating part: if you haven't recognized and identified these underlying beliefs you could be manifesting the exact opposite of what you want. You might *consciously* say you want abundance, but those beliefs will subconsciously continue to guide your actions, creating a cycle of financial self-sabotage.

You might *say* "money is good," but if your core belief is that "money is bad," you will continue to repel money instead of attracting it. Until it's addressed, that belief will do everything in its power to keep you at the level of existence you've always known.

That is the definition of a manifesting block, and holy crap do they *suck*!

Truthfully, this is the block that held me back my whole life. It's the one I did the most work to remove, and the one that still surfaces from time to time. It can be the most frustrating one of all, because nobody wants to work their ass off on their hustle, only to find out they've been blocking the financial rewards of all that work. It sucks! Take it from me.

But lucky for you, I've put in the work and learned how to remove this block, not just for myself but also for countless clients, so that you can do it too.

"But I Can't Afford It!"

One of the reasons the "broke" mindset is the biggest blocker for most people is because your brain has a difficult time dreaming of, or wanting, things you can't currently "afford." For example: The thought pops into your brain: "Oh, wouldn't it be fun to drink champagne while gazing up at the Eiffel Tower in Paris, or take my family on a cruise, or sit front row at a Beyoncé concert, or stand in the Coliseum in Rome, or (insert your 'crazy' dreams here)." Your brain responds with "I can't afford that right now, so why think about it?" And just like that, your dream is kiboshed and the thought is immediately banished.

homework

What are some of your known beliefs about money? Answer the following question honestly ten times in your journal with one-word answers.

- Money is...
- Money is...
- Money is...
- Money is...
- Money is...
- Money is...
- Money is...
- Money is...
- Money is...
- Money is...

This is how you eliminate the "broke" mindset:

Tip 1: Stop Talking about Money!

Have you ever noticed how broke people always talk about money? Either they are talking about how broke they are, or complaining about how things are "too expensive" and how they "can't afford things," or trash-talking people who have money, or constantly stressing about their bills and checking their bank account ten times a day.

If this is you, STOP! Just knock it off!

The more you talk about anything, the bigger it gets, *good or bad*. So if you're bitching about not having money, the only result you will ever receive is *less money*! The Universe delivers what you focus on. *Please* let this be a lightbulb moment! If all day long you are focusing on how little money you have, then common sense says "Less money is on its way." And I'm willing to bet that's not the outcome you're after!

The fastest way to improve your financial situation and change a "broke" mindset is to *stop talking about money*! Just zip it!

Tip 2: Change Your Thinking

I cover this concept in great detail in my book *Hustle, Believe, Receive*, but it's so important that I couldn't address the issue of money without mentioning it here. Your thoughts are predicting your future as we speak. In this very moment, what you've thought about today will show up in the weeks, months, and years to come. That's just the way it is. It's a fact of life, the very essence of the Law of Attraction. Your thoughts are forming your words, your words are creating your actions, and your actions are producing your outcomes. It's a simple formula. Your thoughts are either the foundation for change or the culprit for stagnation and repeated negative cycles.

As long as your thoughts say things like: "I can't afford that." "I don't have enough money." "That's too expensive." Those statements will *always be your reality.*

Process that. Let it marinate! It's intense, I know.

When I first realized this, it felt like a crushing blow. *Say what? I was responsible for my financial situation!?* That was a hard pill to swallow, especially when on the surface it all seemed circumstantial and beyond my control. I'd always thought (financially at least) life seemed stacked against me. Endlessly I stressed about not having enough money. Then when our home foreclosed it *wasn't my fault, it was the market's. We were just victims of bad luck in a real estate bubble.* I never stopped to consider that maybe I shouldn't have bought that house in the first place. Maybe I should have kept that down payment in my savings account a little longer. My fear of "not having enough money" mani-fested in us *not having enough money* to keep our home. It manifested in my making decisions that would make sure we didn't *have enough money* (buying the house when we really couldn't afford it). See, our thoughts are constantly guiding our decisions. They ensure our out-comes always match the thought. So guard your mind! Be relentless at replacing these negative voices in your head with the outcome you *want.*

Offense and Defense

Think of your mind as a basketball court on which there are two teams playing against each other. The winning team is the one with the best offense *and* defense. You need both skills to win.

For example: If your thought is saying "I never have money to do the things I want to do or stay financially ahead," then you should play defense.

PLAY DEFENSE

When that negative thought arises, think of it as the opponent trying to score. You don't just stand there, right? You try to defend the basket (your positive mindset). Got the visual? Great, now every single time these thoughts creep in, replace them with the motto: "There is always *more than* enough to provide for myself and my family. Abundance is already on its way!"

This is how you play mental defense to change your thoughts. You replace an old thought (one that no longer serves you) with a new motto that counters the old belief and claims a new desired outcome.

At first your brain will protest and try to object, reminding you that these new positive statements are *not* your current reality. "It's a lie!" your brain might be yelling. But listen, your brain doesn't know the difference between truth and a lie when repeated over time. There are many scientific studies (Thinkers, go check them out online, there are tons!) that prove the brain quickly adapts when you tell it a lie. With repetition, your mind will overwrite the truth with the new lie. So why wouldn't you use this to your greatest advantage?

"There is always more than enough."

The more times you use these positive mottos and focus on the outcomes you want, the quicker your brain will begin to believe them as true and that faster you will begin manifesting. Over time, your brain will get fed up with the internal argument, and those negative thoughts will begin decreasing. When they recede, and positivity takes their place, you are much more motivated to make shit happen! The more motivated you are, the more work you put in. The more you hustle for what you want, the faster you get it. It's all connected.

Can you see how a motto (even one that didn't feel real at first) sets off a positive domino effect? How a thought has the power to impact motivation, actions, words, beliefs, hustle, and ultimately get you desired results? It's so powerful.

This pattern has been at work in your life already, whether you knew it or not. Unknowingly, you could have been using this formula backward! Let me demonstrate what it looks like in reverse. This might help you see that your life today is a reflection of your previous thoughts.

Formula in reverse: When you allow negative thoughts, they grow. When they grow you are less motivated to take action. When you don't take action, you feel like crap. When you feel crappy you are vulnerable to experiencing depression, stagnation, stress, and anxiety. When you feel that way, you tend to focus on it and it grows even bigger. The bigger it gets the more you begin to *believe* it as an absolute, unchangeable truth. When you believe it to be true, you will *always* manifest it, making it true.

It's a dangerous hamster wheel. If you've been on it, or are currently riding that vicious cycle, here's the second tool in your arsenal to get you off that ride.

PLAY OFFENSE

Several times a day you need to *proactively* tell yourself the story of the person you *want to become* and the life you *want to live.*

homework

Write five power mottos about money that will help you change your subconscious beliefs. Say them every single day, morning and night, until you *believe* them with every fiber of your being. When you do, write five more that seem "unbelievable," and so on. This is not a destination; it's *always* a moving target. What you tell yourself with repetition becomes your core belief, so implant the outcome you want!

Here are a few examples, but write ones that feel powerful to you.

- "I am worthy and ready to receive financial abundance."
- "I deserve and am receiving success and prosperity!"
- "Wealth and abundance are my reward for all this hustle. It is already in progress!"
- "There is *always* more than enough money and prosperity for me."

This means that you are not solely playing defense. This is *huge* by the way. Most self-help teachings only touch on the defense part, but without the offense you won't really be changing your story and creating your desired future outcomes.

By offensively thinking about your new life throughout the day, you are combating future negativity, keeping it at bay, and speeding up its recession. You are also creating a positive, happy, mental refuge from the realities of your world. Make daydreaming a constant practice. Allow yourself to slip off into this peaceful new "happy place" as often as possible.

Make daydreaming a constant practice.

I have intentionally, with lots of practice, made this my mental resting state. I've trained my mind to go to this happy place when I'm doing mindless tasks like driving, cleaning the house, exercising, or anytime I need a quick escape. It's this ability to proactively focus on the life I'm creating and the moments I want to experience, rather than dwelling on the stress of my current realities, that has been so life changing for me. It's one of the fastest ways to speed up manifesting.

Pro tip: Always use present tense when referring to anything you want. Say "I am" instead of "I want" or "I will." Claim it. Implant that new story as if it's a given. As if it's promised to you. Then *always* follow that declaration by saying "thank you." Thank God or the Universe for hearing and for conspiring on your behalf to make it true.

Tip 3: Separate the Dream from the Money

We are conditioned to think of *everything* in terms of *What does it cost?* and *Can I afford it?* But it's important to separate your dreams from money. They are *not* the same thing. You must first have the dream (probably long before you "have the money") in order for any of this to work. Without the dream you'll remain stagnant, your life will not move forward, and you'll miss all these beautiful moments that are dying to come into your life. Until you remove money from the equation, you can't properly dream big because it will always hold you back.

The most magical part about manifesting using my method is that many of the biggest moments I've ever received didn't cost me a thing! That's right, most of the once-in-a-lifetime, insane manifestations from my #FutureBoard were absolutely *free*.

Personal Example #1 (Cost = $0)

In October of 2016, I manifested a three-week trip for myself and my children to Italy (more on how I pulled that off later). It was day four of our trip, and we'd excitedly boarded the train from Venice to Verona for our first little excursion. As we pulled into Verona, the song "Only Fools Rush In" by Andrea Bocelli began to play on the train. It just so happens that's our family's favorite song, one I've played for my children since infancy. I've been listening to the butter voice of Bocelli since my early twenties and my kids have grown up with him as the soundtrack to their childhood. They looked at me in surprised disbelief. "Mama! Are you playing that on your phone again?" they asked. But I wasn't. It was an announcement over the intercom saying Bocelli was performing that night at the amphitheater in Verona!

God! I wish we could go, I thought. But our plan was to visit a cliffside ancient monastery, forty-five minutes outside the city. When we arrived at the train station in Verona we were disappointed to discover that getting to the monastery was an unexpected ordeal, one we couldn't manage.

"Now what?" The kids looked at me expectantly, wrongfully assuming I had a backup plan. "Can we go to the concert?" they chirped. Off we went to Verona's city center in search of adventure and the remote possibility I could wrangle tickets for that evening's concert.

No luck. It turns out Bocelli is from Verona and this was a big deal. Paparazzi flooded the streets and red carpets and step-and-repeat celebrity photo ops marked the entrances to the ancient open-air amphitheater in the center of town. The tickets had long since sold out.

Oh, well, just being in the city of love on such a festive occasion was good enough for us. We lunched gazing at the coliseum, we left a note for Juliet under her balcony, and strolled the pristine streets. As we rounded a corner toward the amphitheater, music suddenly filled the air. The unmistakable voice of Andrea Bocelli drifted like a movie score down the side streets, engulfing us. As we moved closer, passing a side entrance with an unobstructed view of the stage, there he stood. His eyes closed, that unmistakable voice pouring into the microphone. I kid you not. He was conducting a sound check, singing "Only Fools Rush In," paparazzi snapping pictures of his every move.

Manifesting often exceeds your wildest expectations.

The kids and I froze. Tears blurred my view. My heart burst with such insane, full-body joy. We looked at each other in utter amazement. We could see him! He was singing *our song*!

That intimate, unforgettable moment didn't cost a penny. It's one I could have never orchestrated, even if I'd tried. Manifesting often exceeds your wildest expectations. It frequently surprises and always delights. It delivers moments and experiences we could never line up ourselves. The Universe knew what it was doing when it gave us the idea to go to

Verona. It made the monastery trip impossible, it made sure our favorite singer "just so happened" to be in *that town*, on *that day*, singing *that song*. It's beyond comprehension. If you follow the recipe for manifesting in this book, you'll experience firsthand how the Universe is always lining things up behind the scenes in a way that will blow you mind!

P.S. This was not a one-off manifestation for me. Since 2010, when I first learned these skills, I've experienced countless, unbelievable *free* moments just like this. Including court-side seats at NBA games, box seats to Yankees and Knicks games, flying first class, stays at the Ritz-Carlton, and a brand-new Gucci bag and Louboutin shoes! Yep, you read correctly, everything I just mentioned did not cost me a single cent. And there have been so many others, too many to name. It's a thrilling, glorious way of life, I can tell you! You don't need to be rich to start living like you are! If you'd like to see the story and photos behind any of the previous manifestations check out my "REALITY Board" on *Pinterest*.

Personal Example #2 (Cost = $179)

Kanen is my kind, gentlehearted son. In 2010, when he was seven years old, I asked if he'd like to tell me his wildest dream. I was making my second #FutureBoard, after having manifested about 70 percent of the first one in just under two years, and wanted my new board to reflect his dreams as well as mine.

"If you could do anything in the whole wide world, what would it be?" I asked him. I was having one of those proud, pat yourself on the back kinda parenting moments, telling my son how all his dreams were possible. We'd just watched the movie *The Blind Side* with Sandra Bullock, featuring the story of Michael Oher, and as it happens we are die-hard Ravens fans (the team Michael Oher played for at the time).

Kanen looked at me with hopeful, excited eyes and said, "Mama, I want to go to a Ravens game in Baltimore. And I want to meet Michael Oher!" My heart sank. *Crap!* I thought. *How the hell am I going to make that happen?*

Now let me just stop the story for a moment to say that at this point I was still a struggling single mom. It had been a little over two years since my husband left and I was desperately trying to get my bearings financially. By this time, I'd manifested some pretty amazing things from my first #FutureBoard, including a big title promotion at work, but the money situation was still tight. Plus, there was the little matter of: we lived in Portland, Oregon, and the Ravens were in Baltimore, Maryland...a near impossibility in my budget.

But the Universe works in mysterious ways once our heart's desire is made known.

This was a ridiculous ask of the Universe, I thought. But what could I say to my optimistic little boy? "Oh, oops, sorry son. I meant only *realistic* dreams!" Yeah, that wasn't going to happen.

So I smiled at him reassuringly, and together we picked out a picture of the Ravens' M&T Bank Stadium to add to my board. Thankfully, I took the board to work where it inspired and motivated me, propped up in my cubicle. Being out of sight, Kanen luckily seemed to forget about it, easing my mommy guilt about overpromising and under-delivering.

But the Universe works in mysterious ways once our heart's desire is made known (thus the reason I made you make your list), and roughly nine months later I began life coaching a retired Ravens player. One day he casually mentioned that if I ever wanted to take Kanen to a game in Baltimore, that he'd be happy to arrange the tickets.

Immediately I recognized this suggestion as an *opportunity* (we'll learn more about those later) but thought, *How can I possibly afford a cross-country trip?* Not to mention I'd recently made a foolish career move that resulted in my being unexpectedly laid off—the timing couldn't have been worse. But I frantically checked my frequent flier miles anyway hoping for a miracle, and to my astonishment I had exactly enough for two round trip tickets to Baltimore.

A few weeks later Kanen and I were picking up our tickets at will call and were shocked to see that we'd been upgraded to field passes! (P.S. The Universe likes to surprise us with little reminders that we could have dreamed even bigger, because its potential to deliver amazingness beyond anything we could have imagined is endless.)

One of the purest, most joy-filled moments of my life was watching my son's face as we walked out the team tunnel onto the field where the Ravens were running through pregame warm-ups. It's one thing to manifest something *we want*, it's a whole other to manifest it for our children or someone we love. The joy of that moment still gives me goose bumps, and to this day when I tell this story to audiences around the country, I get all choked up.

I look over at Kanen as we walk down the field. I'm sneaking a quick video of the moment when he starts frantically patting my arm.

"Mama! Mama! Mama!" he says, voice cracking in excitement. "There's Michael Oher!" He points across the field where Michael is stretching with enormous headphones around his neck. We stand on the sidelines staring as Michael slowly crosses the field, headed in our general direction. People are yelling at him, calling his name, hoping he'll look in their direction for a quick photo or glance of recognition.

He walks directly up to my son, puts out his hand to shake Kanen's, and says, "So I hear you've been looking for me!"

home work

Can you think of a time when you experienced something amazing and it didn't cost you much (or any) money? We've all had them, you just probably didn't recognize it as a manifestation.

Finding examples in your own life enables you to see how the process has worked in the past and it gives you faith. So now that you have the formula for how to really master this moving forward, prepare yourself to be amazed! Oh! And don't try to say this hasn't happened to you, because I can promise you it has. If you can't spot one at first, it's because you're not looking hard enough or are not grateful for it now or when it happened. Gratitude is what makes these moments come alive! Think harder.

Maybe it was an experience with a friend that they paid for? Or maybe you won it? Maybe it was something awesome you experienced through your job? Maybe it was a gift? Maybe it was a once-in-a-lifetime moment that wasn't something you needed to "buy"?

Write about it in your journal. Try to remember the details of how it came about and how you felt in the moment. Did it make you happy? Did you feel joy? Was it unexpected?

Now do you see what I mean? You're about to *create* a ton more!

Summary

In this chapter you learned how to recognize if a "broke" mindset is blocking you from manifesting the financial success you desire. You also learned to spot the various ways it influences your beliefs, which have in turn created your past outcomes.

You learned three simple ways to begin changing this mindset:

1. Stop talking about money.

2. Change your thinking about money by applying the tools of playing offense and defense.

3. Separate the dream from the money and find examples in your life of manifesting without money.

One of the most important concepts of this chapter is that *you* control your thoughts and those thoughts control your outcomes. You learned that your mind believes what you tell it, so you should use this fact to your greatest advantage.

If money has been a hang-up for you in the past, I suggest you come back to the homework in this section often. Reread the tools in each tip until you understand how to apply them in various situations in your life with success. They really will work, but it's up to you to use them.

I want you to receive all the financial rewards of your hard work, and all the monetary success you deserve. This chapter will help you ensure that you do!

03: WHAT'S BLOCKING YOU? CHANGING THE "I'M NOT WORTHY" MINDSET

This chapter will tackle the second block to manifesting: the "I'm not worthy" mindset. It is one of those blocks that has deep roots in your subconscious beliefs, and is sometimes tricky to spot because it's often quickly dismissed. On the surface it's easy to reject this block as irrelevant, because it's difficult to admit you might feel unworthy. And consciously, it might *not* be how you feel right now. But again, your pesky subconscious usually runs the show. It may be clinging to old, deeply buried beliefs that find their roots in your childhood. And though buried, those beliefs can still direct your outcomes until they're eradicated.

The work in this chapter is important even if you don't think this block is relevant to you—it still may uncover unknown blocks that when removed can enable you to begin manifesting the life you want.

Identifying the "Unworthy" Mindset

The "I'm not worthy" mindset is the belief (conscious or subconscious) that you don't deserve abundance, wealth, love, or a fabulous life. One of the reasons "unworthiness" is so tricky to diagnose in yourself is because it shows up in other, more subtle forms. On the surface you can tell yourself you are worthy of all the amazing things life has in store for you, but if these other behaviors are present in your life, "unworthiness" is still affecting your results, or lack thereof. The two primary ways this belief reveals itself are in the forms of self-sabotage and fear.

The Art of Self-Sabotage

"Unworthiness" often shows up in the form of self-sabotage. Whenever something seems to be going really well for us, we start to question it. An old nasty voice inside us says "It's too good to be true. It can't last. Nothing good ever lasts." Or "The person we love will leave us, just like everyone else has." Or "I'm just waiting for the other shoe to drop." All of these beliefs fall into the category of believing you are not worthy or deserving of the good things life has to offer. These deeply rooted beliefs, some of which you've carried for a lifetime, have been calling the shots in your life. They determine your actions, which of course produce results that back up those beliefs.

For example: Take the underlying belief that "people you love, leave you." This belief is probably based on personal life experience. You've likely seen it play out in your life several times, maybe starting as early as childhood. If you are carrying this belief, what happens then when the love of your life shows up?

Everything is going great, you're blissfully happy, then all of a sudden, an old negative thought based in this belief begins to eat away at your happiness. It replaces your joy with doubt, which turns into many other things. Maybe jealousy? Maybe possessiveness? Maybe meanness and nagging? It begins manifesting in all these other forms, because what you *believe* is what you *manifest*. So if you believe that you are not worthy and deserving of blissful, happy love, you will take actions to sabotage that love and drive that person away. You will have manifested the demise of the very thing you wanted.

Manifesting can happen in positive and negative ways.

See, manifesting can happen in positive *and* negative ways. You are always manifesting what you believe and that is why it's so critical to uncover these beliefs and change them. Believing that you are not worthy of success, wealth, prosperity, love, a loving family, good friends, and a beautiful life will repel those things from you. That's why we call them blocks, because they literally stand between you and what you want.

Fear Is a Dream Killer

"Unworthiness" also shows up in the form of fear. When things are going well and you are starting to get what you want, what emotion often rears its ugly head? Fear. It may take the form of a lump in the pit of your stomach, or anxiety, or stress. If those emotions ever pop up when you are happy or when things are going well, you need to recognize them for what they truly are: self-sabotaging blockers to everything you want.

homework

Grab your journal and take note of any recognizable negative patterns in your life. We all have them. For some it might be relationships, career, or money. Still others might self-sabotage their health or weight. Maybe it's procrastination or avoidance? What are your areas of self-sabotage? Write about a few times in your life where you can see a pattern reappear. For me, money was always an area of self-destruction, so when I took inventory of my past results, it wasn't hard to spot the pattern. Once you've identified a few examples, think back to what you may have been thinking when those patterns began. What thoughts started them? Write them down.

Now that you've been able to identify some of these thoughts, you'll recognize them much faster when they creep up in the future. There are three tools to changing these thoughts in the following section of this chapter. Apply them to shut down past distractive thoughts, which will put an end to this pattern.

Note: This is a practice, not a one-time solution. You will become more accurate at identifying and changing these patterns the more you apply these tools. So be diligent.

They arise because their job is to keep you from breaking out of your comfortable box. They are present for the sole purpose of holding you back and keeping you down.

How to Remove Your "Unworthy" Thoughts

Here are simple ways to change and remove your thoughts of unworthiness, so you can begin receiving abundance.

- **First, recognize the thought without emotional attachment.** When negative thoughts and fear arise bringing their entourage of stress and anxiety, the first step is to remove yourself emotionally from them. Look at the thought objectively. Ask yourself, "Does this thought serve me? Is it going to get me closer to living my dreams or is it here to keep me from them?" By doing this, you stop these thoughts in their tracks, removing their power.

- **Second, decide if you want the thought to be true for you.** Every thought you think is subjective. It is up to you to add value, weight, and "truth" to it. It is your *choice* if you want to believe old thoughts or not. Just because you've thought or believed something your entire life, does not make it true. You can decide, right now, to debunk those thoughts if they no longer serve you. So look at it from an outsider's perspective, and ask the question "Do I want this to be true, for me, moving forward?" If the answer is no, then stop accepting it as truth! Stop giving it value and weight.

- **Third, DO NOT engage!** The key to changing old beliefs is to *not* entertain them. Don't allow an internal conversation to begin or continue, it will only take you down a rabbit hole. If you've asked the previous question if you want this thought to be true for you and the answer was no, then shut this thought down immediately! Do not give it air to breathe and grow. Do not argue with it. Do not give it validation or the time of day. You've decided it no longer serves you, so you are *done*!

- **Lastly, change the subject.** Our brains have the attention span of a two-year-old with ADHD, so this trick isn't difficult to use. Just like a child might throw a tantrum when you take away his toy (like you not engaging in negative old thoughts), he can usually be appeased by replacing the old toy with a shiny new one (thoughts about your dreams). So immediately change the subject in your brain by thinking of your dream future life. Begin imagining a specific piece of that life, a part that you know will be easy and pleasurable to focus on for a few minutes. And just like a toddler, your brain will soon forget its tantrum and happily play with its new toy!

Immediately change the subject in your brain by thinking of your dream future life.

Remember that these emotions and thoughts are tricky little bastards! They have lived with you for a long time and are quite comfortable with their position of guiding (or destroying) your life, so they won't go without a fight. For a while, they will come at you in new and creative ways, making it harder to objectively recognize them for what they are, so be on guard. Also, be kind to yourself—if you miss one or two along the way it's okay. Just commit to always improving and practicing what you've just learned and eventually those thoughts will diminish.

homework

Have you struggled with feelings of unworthiness? Where did they come from? Think back to your earliest memory of when you felt like you didn't deserve something good. Grab your journal and write about it. Who told you that you didn't deserve it?

Throughout your life who's told you that you don't deserve to have it all? Whose are those voices and what do they say? We aren't born feeling unworthy, that's a belief that is instilled in us over time and one that we perpetuate in various ways throughout our life. It's important to find the answers to these questions. Once we know them, then we are able to remove their power and change our beliefs moving forward. So get real with yourself, uncover the truth.

Putting It Into Action

Back to the earlier example of "people you love, leave you."

The first sign of your old blocking belief may have been the thought "what if they leave me?" Or "what if this doesn't work out?" The first time this thought entered your consciousness you had a choice: you could either continue engaging with it *or* you could instantly and objectively recognize it for the sabotaging belief that it was and stomp it out.

If you let it grow, what happens? It's not long before you start building all kinds of worst-case fictional scenarios in your mind about the various ways that person can leave you, hurt you, cheat on you, you name it! Suddenly the one you love becomes a suspect, someone you need to guard yourself against. That thought turns into fear, which turns to anxiety and becomes an ongoing source of stress, until you finally wind up destroying something that could have been beautiful.

On the other hand, if you pay attention to your thoughts you can notice when an irrational or destructive one is trying to get in. Now you recognize it, so instead of letting it get carried away like you would have in the past, you say, "You know what? You are bullshit. I see you trying to ruin a good thing and I'm over your running my life! Your day has come. I run the show now! That old belief no longer serves me. It does *not* get me what I want. You are not winning this time!" And after that long-overdue tongue-lashing to the devil on your shoulder, you can give him a firm brushing off, put your head up in pride, and stomp off slamming the door behind you!

Summary

In this chapter you learned that the feeling of unworthiness often appears in disguise. It can come in:

1. The form of self-sabotage

2. The form of fear and anxiety

You then learned simple tools for identifying these patterns, thoughts, and behaviors, and discovered easy ways to remove them. Including:

● Recognizing the initial thoughts with emotional detachment.

● Deciding if you want those thoughts to be true for you.

● Not engaging those thoughts.

● And finally, you learned that to change them permanently, you must change the subject in your brain each time they arise.

If this block is one that really resonated with you, be gentle with yourself. It can be an emotional land mine and might take several passes at this homework to really dig deep enough to uncover and remove all these old, limiting beliefs.

It is a process. I've found that people (like me) who've come from a financially difficult (I was dirt poor) childhood often really struggle with "unworthiness." If you can relate, then just do your best now, apply what you've learned, and come back to it in a few months. You'll find you'll be able to take it one level deeper then.

Pro tip: I have also used Reiki energy healing to help me release some of these deeply buried subconscious beliefs and it's done wonders! If that's something you're open to, ask your friends or your social media for a recommendation of someone who's really good, and do three to five sessions while you are doing this work. The combination of both together is so powerful!

04: WHAT'S BLOCKING YOU? CHANGING THE "LOW-KEY MARTYR" MINDSET

This final block is tricky. Unlike the previous two, I don't consider it an actual "belief," it's more of a surface deflection, a defense mechanism, or a mask for the true underlying block. I've coached many people with this mindset over the years and I must admit, it's one of the toughest to penetrate. Because when someone's using this excuse, they are normally very defensive and their mind is closed to this process. I've successfully walked almost everyone through this, but it takes time and patience to help someone with this block realize that it is a block. That it's really nothing more than an excuse to not dream. I'll walk you through how to identify it, and then how to move past it. Be open...the results will make all this work so worth it!

Identifying the "Low-Key Martyr" Mindset

The "low-key martyr" mindset is the superficial belief that you "don't need" anything big or fancy; that your dreams and life are simple and you're just fine with that. The "low-key martyr" is always saying things like: "Oh, I don't need all that fancy stuff. I like my life, I'm good. That stuff (wealth, abundance, luxury, travel, the good life) is not for me." To which I will always ask the obvious question: "Then why are you wasting your money hiring me as your coach? If your life is great right now and you already have everything you want, why are we having this conversation?"

One of the most common underlying blockers for this mindset is often rooted in religious or faith-based beliefs. Many organized religions teach that wealth, or living a life that would be deemed "lavish," is sinful or "bad." Therefore the desire to live an abundant life can conflict with these beliefs even if the person is no longer religious, leaving them feeling torn and defensive.

I say this with firsthand knowledge. I was raised in a radical, offshoot branch of the Seventh-day Adventist Church. These were beliefs my parents held and drilled into me from infancy. Beliefs that: *Having financial wealth was evil. That God punishes the rich. That the meek would inherit the earth*…and on and on. Even though I stopped being "religious" at age sixteen, those beliefs persisted throughout my life, and I've had to work overtime to correct them. So I get it. Creating an abundant, full, gorgeous, and luxurious life can incite the defensive response: "Oh, that's just not me."

But you know what? I don't buy it. I don't believe that there is anyone out there who would *hate* to go on a beautiful luxury vacation with his or her family. I don't think there's anyone who would *hate* to have

homework

Is it easier for you to think of things to do for others than yourself? Why? Grab your journal and start writing. Get to the root of that question, honestly. Why is it so hard? What do you feel when you think of doing nice things for yourself? Identify the feeling. Guilt? Selfishness? Narcissism? Judgment? Fear? What is it? Once you identify the underlying feeling or emotion, it's much easier for you to debunk them as myths, creating a new story for yourself. You've gotta let them go, before you can move on to creating the life you want.

a gorgeous kitchen where they can cook for their family and friends in homey luxury. I don't think there's anyone who would turn down a chance to take a selfie in front of the Eiffel Tower if it was given to them. I just don't. I think there are lots of people out there who will say they don't need any of that, or they don't want it, but it's not true. It's a cop-out.

Usually what's buried underneath is a combination of these:

- They're afraid they really *do* want it.

- They're afraid people will judge them for wanting it.

- They're afraid wanting it will make them "selfish" or "a bad person."

- They're afraid someone in their life will not approve of them wanting more for their life.

- They're afraid to be disappointed.

- They think wanting it will mean they aren't grateful for what they have.

Saying they "don't need it" is easier than admitting they can't afford it, or don't feel worthy, or don't believe they could ever have it, or don't know how to get it, or risking disappointment if they don't get it. These underlying reasons are the ones we want to get to; they are the ones that need to be recognized and changed.

Another manifestation of this mindset is the reaction "I just want to help people." This shows up when I ask them "What do you want?" And all the responses have to do with other people. None (or few) of the answers are about them personally. And while this seems really noble, it's actually another deflection. It's a way to avoid answering the question for *themselves*, because they have no idea what they want.

Virginia Jennings
CALIFORNIA, USA

"I am living my dream life."

My story begins on October 19, 2015. That's the date of my first coaching session with Sarah. She asked me to begin the process by writing down exactly where I was in my life at the time. She insisted I write by hand in a journal and she was right; something special happens when it flows off the pen.

I wrote about each of the five core areas of my life (relationships, career, financial, body, and mind). At the time I had a job I hated that I'd been in for over seven years. It was an incredibly toxic environment. My relationship of eight years had crumbled, and my divorce had just become official. I had dated, but hated it. I didn't know what I wanted, but I knew I did want to be in a relationship again. Financially, I'd just filed bankruptcy and had used what was left of my savings to hire Sarah as my coach. Physically, I've always struggled with my weight and health. Spiritually, I was searching, watching astrological videos for comfort and strength through all of this.

I wrote in my journal that I hoped doing all this work would change things for me. I felt "lame" because I didn't have any wonderful goals or big dreams.

At the end of this homework assignment I wrote these words:

- I am divorced and alone.
- I am bankrupt and broke.
- I have a job that I hate most days.
- I am overweight and out of shape.
- I feel disconnected and sad.

I began working through the homework assignments with Sarah, sometimes even feeling detached from them. But I learned it was okay, as long as I did the work anyway. So I wrote openly and honestly so I could be honest with, and accountable to, myself. Through this work, I realized how much my fear and negative thinking were holding me back, and how much the Universe really does provide.

One of my very first manifestations, just a few weeks after beginning this journey, was when my car was involved in a fender bender and sent to the shop. At first I was so frustrated because I was financially struggling, and it seemed like just another "bad thing" had happened to me.

But then I realized that I'd wanted to take a road trip to see my daughter and grandson, but couldn't because my car was not four-wheel drive and the roads were covered in snow. Lo and behold, my insurance got me a rental car with a free upgrade to four-wheel drive! Wow! The Universe was already providing!

One thing Sarah taught me that really made things shift in my life was writing positive mottos and claiming them as my future outcomes. This took multiple tries. It feels weird at first, but don't give up.

These were some of my original mottos, they were the inspiration for the pictures I put on my #FutureBoard:

- I live with my best friend and we are smitten with each other. We perfectly complement each other.

- We have an extremely comfortable income that provides more than enough for my partner and me.

- We are both physically active, walking and riding bikes, eating healthy.

● Our home is over 1,800 square feet, open and sunny with a hot tub and a swimming pool, the birds are chirping and it's warm and lovely. The home is stucco, light, airy, and open. Creamy colors make up the decor. The living room is open to the kitchen. The pool and backyard are private and beautiful!

After getting through my first Christmas alone in 2015, the most wonderful thing happened. I met Gary, the love of my life, on January 20, 2016. I knew immediately that he was *the* one. We started dating and soon became inseparable.

He was retired and would often say, "Your work thing is cramping my style!" I still hated my job. Well, I learned that Sarah was right, you get what you focus on! In April of 2016 I was terminated from my job. At first, this seemed like a real blow. It changed things significantly. All of a sudden I had no income. I was going to have to draw unemployment for the first time in my life (at the age of fifty-six). But I soon learned that it was a blessing in disguise.

Being unemployed allowed me to convert my bankruptcy from a Chapter 13 (where I was paying it back at high monthly payments) to a Chapter 7, getting rid of my high monthly payments. I was able to keep my house and its equity, but all the rest of my debts were now gone! This was a *huge* manifestation.

On July 1, 2017, Gary and I got married in sunny Palm Springs, California. It was time for us to manifest our biggest dream of moving from snowy, cold Eastern Washington State to sunny California. We both sold our homes for a good profit and we were *off*! We looked at several homes in San Diego before we found *the one*, the home of our dreams that was on my #FutureBoard! We have a pool, have added a hot tub, we have an exercise room with a treadmill and we do yoga in the mornings together. We now ride our bikes together down by the beach. We both also have motorcycles.

All of this stuff was on my #FutureBoard! I remember telling Sarah that I felt "lame" because my board and dreams didn't seem to include "work."

"That's okay," she'd said. "Focus on creating the future life that makes *you* happy."

It's all crystal clear now. Two years after beginning my work with Sarah, I am retired at age fifty-eight, with money in the bank and no debt! I am living my dream life with my best friend and husband! I live in my dream home in a dream location, living an active, healthy lifestyle.

If you had asked me when I started this journey if I would be here now, I never could have even imagined it. Do the homework assignments! Write in your journal. Make your #FutureBoard. My life has done a complete 180 since I learned how to manifest with Sarah's method.

If this sounds like you, take heart! It's very common. Many of us have been raised to believe we should do everything for everyone else and put ourselves last, so in a way these responses are human nature for us, especially for women. Honestly, we moms are the worst! We can write lists a mile long about what everyone in our family wants and what we'd do to help their dreams come true, but we really struggle when the question is about *us*. It can be very emotional. I've conducted many workshops where women have completed the previous homework assignment and realized that nothing on their list was actually about them.

You can be filled with gratitude for what you have and still want and deserve more.

Somewhere along the way, many of us have been conditioned to falsely believe that if we want more, we are being selfish. Or that wanting more means we aren't grateful for what we have. But neither of those is true. You can be filled with gratitude for what you have and still want and *deserve* more. I don't believe that the Universe, or God, created us to struggle. I believe we were created to be abundant. The more abundant we are, the more we can bless the world around us; that doesn't make us bad. It makes us aware and eager to grow into our full potential.

Summary

In this chapter you learned how to penetrate the superficial deflection of the "low-key martyr." You've discovered how to identify if this defense mechanism is rooted in religious beliefs, other people's opinions, or your own fear of wanting more.

You've learned that this block is merely resistance to uncovering the truth about what is really holding you back. And you've answered some tough questions to help you push past this barrier to get the life you want.

Most importantly, I want you to know, that wanting more is *not* selfish, narcissistic, evil, mean, horrible, sinful, or any of those awful things you might have previously thought. It simply means you love yourself *too*. You matter! Your opinions, wants, and dreams are just as important as everyone else's. It does not make you greedy or ungrateful. It does not make you a bad person. People in your life may (and probably will) judge you. You might even lose friends and relationships as a result of taking a stand for what you want, but that is also part of this process. It's part of ensuring that you are choosing the life you want. Don't fear these losses. If people leave your life based on your decision and desire to live your dreams, then those are not people who should be in your life in the first place. The Universe will never leave you lonely. When those people exit, new ones will fill the void. Be willing to make choices that ensure you are surrounded by people who love and support this new direction.

05: BLOWING UP THE BOX

This chapter is all about removing the boundaries that keep you from dreaming HUGE and teaches you how to begin imagining your life in a whole new way. This is such a critical part of building your new life, but it can be a difficult task for many. Dreamers tend to love this part; Thinkers—not so much! But learning how to reinvent what your future looks like is the foundational piece of what will become your physical #FutureBoard.

Sometimes all you need is permission to dream big, someone telling you it's okay and showing you how it's done. That is what you'll learn in this chapter. Keep an open mind (especially you Thinkers out there!) and get ready to blow up your previous notions of what is possible for your life. It's time to replace those ideas with a seriously upgraded version of your future!

Breaking Out of Your Box

We live in a box. Invisible, unrecognized walls around our life that determine what is possible for *us,* even if we aren't aware of them. These walls are created from our childhood, our beliefs, the examples we've seen throughout our lifetime, the people we know, and from our own experiences. They define our beliefs of what is possible.

For some of us, this box may be quite big. We might believe we can do "anything," yet still those walls surround us. Because our version of "anything" is still limited. For others, this box may be tiny. We might not have examples of people who live a "better" life than us. We may not believe we can change anything about our life. In either case, there is always this box, a conscious or subconscious limit to what we believe is possible *for us.*

My goal is to help you take a giant wrecking ball and blow that box to smithereens. It won't happen all at once; it will take time. This growth will come in stages. That's why I recommend you redo the homework in this book every year. Because what feels like the biggest dreams imaginable today will seem normal in a year from now, especially after you've manifested some of them. That's how you continue to blow up this box, by doing this work and pushing yourself.

It will probably feel uncomfortable (especially for Thinkers); it might even feel terrifying. Because even though you might not admit it, there's something oddly comforting about your box. Something protective. You know what your limits are, therefore you won't ever be hurt, or disappointed, as long as you live within those walls, *right?* Removing the box altogether leaves you vulnerable, forces you to imagine a life that you've never previously considered, and that can be disconcerting.

But here's the thing: to get big results you've got to make some dramatic changes in your thinking. You've got to push yourself past the comfort zone if you ever want to live this fabulous life you're creating.

Permission to Dream HUGE!

I know it feels uncomfortable, but listen, I need you to go there. I want you to imagine the *impossible*. Imagine the ludicrous. Only then do you have a shot at manifesting it. And isn't a shot worth it? I'll take those odds over zero any day.

I am giving you permission to dream ridiculously HUGE! To push those walls out as far as humanly possible. Whatever your dreams are, begin asking yourself, "What's the *next level* to this dream?" How can you go bigger?

You know the saying *shoot for the stars, so you can reach the moon*? That's exactly what I want you to do. You have to allow the biggest possible version of your dream life to take shape in your mind first, because manifesting happens in stages. Not overnight. It's incremental—if you're dreaming small, you'll manifest minute! And who wants that? So dream HUGE; that way your manifesting increments will be bigger from the start.

Don't be the thing that blocks your abundance, your manifestations, and your happiness. Don't stand in the way of those things flowing into your life. If you're blocking the mere *thought* of abundance, how could you ever *receive* the actual thing?! Give your imagination a chance to conceive of a life that's dramatically different than any you've previously considered, because living those realities is so worth it!

Tips for Thinkers

This is probably tough for you Thinkers. It's all about imagining the impossible, to allow yourself to dream HUGE! This goes against your rational reasoning tendencies and will be difficult at first. But keep pushing yourself, because at a certain point, if you follow the instructions, you'll break free!

If a negative voice pipes up in your head trying to point out all the reasons why this is ridiculous, RESIST!

Let the voice of possibility be heard.

Take a deep breath and say, "I have to dream it first if I ever want to live it. I am allowing myself to dream. I am choosing my dreams over my present reality."

Personal Example

The most outrageous thing I've ever manifested happened in 2014. By this time, I'd manifested two #FutureBoards and was quite honestly struggling for "big dream" ideas to put on my third board in 2012.

I'd already manifested several all-expenses-paid trips to New York, Los Angeles, Las Vegas, and DC, many times flying first class. I'd nearly tripled my corporate salary and overall income. I'd achieved the "dream" title of VP and National Director. I drove a Mercedes. I rocked designer bags and shoes. I was training for a marathon. I'd taken my kids to Disneyland and my son to Hawaii and DC. I'd moved my family from a tiny apartment to a large four-bedroom house. *What else was there?*

How do I dream bigger than all of that?

The life I'd manifested was blowing my mind; it was all happening so fast, I could hardly get my head around it. *How do I dream bigger than all of that?* I pondered this.

Then I had it! I'd add a picture of a woman flying on a private jet. It was the most far-fetched, ridiculous thing I could possibly imagine. Nothing was more "unrealistic" or further from my reach. "I will test the Universe!" I said. And then I let it go. I didn't stress about it, or wonder when it was going to happen; I just released the dream like a little butterfly.

"If and when this ever happens," I thought, "it will be an incredible experience, a moment I'll never forget. If it doesn't, I'll live."

I always tell people when they are debating whether or not to put a picture that feels "ridiculous" on their board that a 1 percent chance of living that dream is better than a zero. So why *wouldn't* you put every dream you can think of on your board!? You'd be crazy not to!

Nine months later, I got a call from my best friend. Who, by the way, I'd manifested the previous year. On my second #FutureBoard I'd put pictures of women friends hanging out together, shopping, and laughing. I needed close, positive friends; it was something my life was desperately lacking at the time. A year later I met Courtney; she's been a sister to me ever since.

But I digress—back to her call that August morning. "Is there any way you can take a few days off work?" she asked, her voice laced with excitement and stressful panic.

"I think so. Why? What's up?" I replied.

That's when she told me her husband (an NBA player) had been traded to an East Coast team. It happened overnight, he was already there, and she needed to pack up their life and move to DC, like *yesterday!* Could I help? she wanted to know. "Of course!" I assured her.

A few days later we'd packed the house, the moving vans had come and gone, and we were loaded down with luggage walking across the tarmac to an idling private jet, the pilot offering to help with our luggage.

It was one of those surreal moments, when you can't help but grin from ear to chin, take a million selfies, and ask yourself, "How is this my life right now!?"

The moral of this story? Don't block your dreams! Who are you to say they are impossible or out of reach? Stop overanalyzing and just set them free.

REAL-LIFE SUCCESS STORY

Ellen Apolinar
TEXAS, USA

> "*I got serious about creating the life I wanted.*"

I found Sarah Centrella through her blog in 2010, when she was just starting to share her story. At the time, I had just separated from my husband of twelve years. We had three small children and I had sole custody of them. It was not easy for me to raise them alone because I was earning only a few dollars in my country, the Philippines.

Sarah's story inspired and encouraged me to try something different in my life. I read every blog she wrote, followed her on social media, and even sent her messages. I started following her advice on how to make a #FutureBoard and created my first one. It had just a few small goals on it because I wanted to see if it really worked, and it did!

In 2014 I got serious about creating the life I wanted when I made my second #FutureBoard. I found all the pictures, ones with every detail, just like Sarah said to do. After just a few months the pictures and dreams began to manifest.

It started with my job. I got my dream job with a very kind and wonderful boss. I enrolled my son in a private school. I was able to make an investment in a house in the Philippines. I met the love of my life in 2016 and got engaged that same year. I also got approved for my US visa, which was one of my biggest dreams. I've traveled throughout and around Asia.

In 2016 when Sarah's first book was published, I immediately went to bookstores in Hong Kong (where I'd moved with my children), but unfortunately it was not available. In my mind I believed I would get it, but I didn't know how. I wrote it as an affirmation and put it on my #FutureBoard. After two months of believing that I would get that book, boom! One day a small package was delivered right in front of my door. It was her book, a surprise gift from a friend in the US. While holding the book that night, I told myself, "I want to meet this lady!" I wrote a note and pinned it to my #Future-Board. It read "I will meet Sarah Centrella! Thank you! Thank you Universe!"

In 2017 I married the love of my life and we moved our family to the United States. We bought a home in Texas with a pool in the backyard. I've already visited fourteen states with still more to come!

Lastly, another big manifestation happened today. Today, November 4, 2018, I met Sarah Centrella in person. I never imagined that I'd manifest meeting her so fast! But she came to Dallas for a #FutureBoard workshop and I immediately bought a ticket. During the class I stood up and told my story. Sarah came over, tears in her eyes, and gave me a huge hug!

My dreams have come true. Now it's time for me to make a new #FutureBoard!

I started crying when Ellen stood up in my Dallas workshop and shared this INSANE manifesting story. It was beyond overwhelming to see this beautiful woman, who'd followed me from the start and was quietly applying this method, share how her life had changed. As she went through her list of manifestations, you could see our mouths drop open in astonishment. The other participants and I looked at her in total amazement. I had no idea she would be there; it was incredible to see her dreams unfolding and to be part of them. It was a moment I will never forget.

And oh, yeah, of course, I signed that same book!

homework

Grab your journal and write down twenty "ridiculous" dreams.
These dreams should scare you! They should also give you butterflies at the mere thought of them possibly materializing. I will let you
have free rein on this one, so no rules (I know, right? I can't believe it
either!). It can be something you want to do, accomplish, experience,
buy, see, visit, a person you want to meet...*no limits!*

Summary

In this chapter you learned how to let go and dream HUGE! You recognized that this process is more difficult for Thinkers than Dreamers, and read some specific tips to allow Thinkers to push past barriers to dreaming big.

The most important part of this chapter is to create a foundation for you to build your dream life upon. That's why pushing your comfort limits is so critical, because your "dream life" should be a dramatic upgrade from what you're living now, since manifesting happens in stages. You've learned why it's important to continue pushing the boundaries of your dreams so they can grow and evolve with you over time.

And finally, the homework you completed in this chapter will become the photos that you'll add to your #FutureBoard in Part Two of this book, so make a mental note to start thinking of those twenty dreams as "images."

06: EXPERIENCES OVER THINGS

This is where my approach to "vision boards" takes a dramatic turn from the masses, and it's the number one reason my #FutureBoards manifest so quickly and accurately. Why? Because they focus on *experiences* and not *things*. Traditional "vision boards" are normally about pulling photos of material things from magazines, but *not* #FutureBoards!

In this chapter you'll learn my number one secret to successfully manifesting: it's all about the experiences and the *life* you want to live. You'll learn why this point is so critical to building a happy, abundant, and successful life. And most importantly, you'll learn *how* to do just that!

What Makes You Happy?

You won't fill your #FutureBoard with pictures of random material things you found in a magazine. Not only does that approach rarely work, it won't bring you genuine, lasting happiness either.

Turning Traditional Thinking on Its Head

When it comes to "success," traditional American thinking says *we work like maniacs, so we can afford to take one "big" vacation every five years.* This type of thinking would have you believe that the purpose of your life is to work hard so you can afford a mortgage, a new car, to send your kids to college, and occasionally "enjoy life" when you retire!

I say *screw that!* Let's toss that idea out and start from scratch. What would happen if you built your life around what made you supremely happy? Around the "enjoy life" part, instead of the "work till you die" part? Around the *experiences* and NOT the *things*?

What would happen if you built your life around what made you supremely happy?

"But wait!" I can hear some of you protesting, "I want the things too!" Don't worry, so do I, and that part is coming, but it's not the piece you build your future life around.

Let's take a moment to imagine what your life could be when created using this thinking. Ask yourself: *What would my life look like if I had all the money in the world, to live life to its absolute maximum? What would I DO? Who would I do it with? How would I make every day count? What makes me feel the most alive? What do rich people DO for vacation and fun? What is my reason for being on this planet? What's my reason for working hard? What does "money" mean to me? How would it give me the freedom to live the life I want?*

Those are the questions this section will help you answer.

Most people consider these experiences a *reward* or a *luxury*. The *one vacation in five years* mentality. But I'm saying, what if your life was built around LIVING like this on a regular basis? When you start with this as your foundation, all the rest of it will come because you will draw it into your life. It will be attracted to the energy you exude from living your happiest life.

It doesn't matter if you are starting with a negative bank account and past due rent as I did, or if you're starting in a better financial position, this process works in both scenarios.

So don't worry about all that material stuff; we'll get to that later. For now, just trust me and start imagining a life filled with *doing* everything you love.

Why Experiences Matter

Why are experiences so important to the success of your #FutureBoard?

- **Experiences teach you to focus on what brings you happiness and joy.** When you build your life around experiences, you are training your mind to seek happiness and receive joy. It's one of the fastest ways for you to tap into a sensation of happiness at any given moment, by thinking of an experience you want to live. When you feel that happiness in your mind, you will soon manifest it in real life. It's the old adage: you get back what you put out. It's how you access the fast track to getting in the "flow" of creating manifesting momentum.

- **Experiences teach you how to connect emotional "feeling" to visualization.** Years ago, when I first began learning about manifesting, I remember hearing people talk about "feeling" something before you received it. I was like, WTF? How does that work exactly? I couldn't find the answer and I didn't understand how I could "feel emotionally connected" to getting a new car when I was still struggling to get the rent paid on time! It didn't make sense to me.

But as soon as I put photos on my wall of places I wanted to *see* and moments I wanted to *live*, suddenly I could form a visual movie in my mind about those experiences that led to an emotional attachment. And "feeling" is an important component of manifesting, but one that's hard to conjure up for material things. Learning how to hone your visualization with emotional attachment skills on experiences will help you transfer those skills to anything else later on.

When you think of living a once-in-a-lifetime experience, it's impossible *not* to visualize it. Name any experience: meeting the person you admire most, zip-lining through a jungle, taking a hot air balloon ride, flying first class, stomping grapes at harvest in Tuscany... anything. Now immediately you begin to *see* it in your mind. That is visualization. It comes naturally to some (most Dreamers), but for others (some Thinkers) it's a difficult skill to learn.

Because visualization is the cornerstone of manifesting it's important you know how to do it, how to transport your mind from your present reality to living a moment vividly in your imagination before it happens. When you do this repeatedly, it will begin to form that all-important emotional attachment.

- **Experiences allow you to visually dream HUGE without all the hang-ups.** By "hang-ups" I mean: But *when* will it happen? *How* will it happen? *How* can I afford it? And so on. Thinkers, you get what I'm saying here. All those questions that are trying to prevent you from allowing a dream to take shape, they are trying to kill it before it happens.

Dreaming of experiences makes them easier to *allow*. I mean, who's to say that you will *never* ride in a hot air balloon? Sometimes our brain's obsessive need to control everything means it can't comprehend that an experience-focused dream isn't hurting anyone. Train yourself to just *let it be*. In letting it breathe, you give it a chance to come find you when the timing is right. On the other hand, dreaming of a multimillion-dollar mansion when you're still renting an apartment conjures up more stress (and depression) than anything.

Personal Example

It was the summer of 2010, I was sitting at my desk staring at the picture on my wall of Hawaii: the waves, the sand, and that damn hammock, which never seemed to stop beckoning me, when I got an email.

By this time, I was working like a maniac, traveling a lot for work, and trying to keep my life together and my career moving up the corporate ladder. We were still in the same apartment, but things had started looking up. I was getting the finances a little more together. I'd started running and was feeling pretty good about myself. I'd even started dating. My focus was:

1. My kids and being the absolute best, most present mom when I wasn't at work.

2. My career. My blog had started taking off as people began noticing how I was turning my life around. I was sharing my wins and losses and people were digging it.

I opened the email; it was a promotion through my preferred airline for a mileage deal to Maui, Hawaii. I stared at it. *I couldn't possibly go to Hawaii!? That would be crazy! Only rich people take vacations to Hawaii and I am NOT RICH.* I went through the list of excuses, all the reasons why there was no way on earth I could go.

But something in me recognized that email as an opportunity. The months of staring at that picture had allowed me to connect the dots enough to entertain the idea for the very first time. And pay attention people…because this is how manifesting works. Then I did something crazy. I decided it couldn't hurt to just *check it out.* So I clicked the link and put in my mileage number. To my total shock I had enough miles saved up from all my recent business travel for two round trip tickets to Maui! I couldn't believe it!

But the skeptic in me unleashed a torrent of fear and doubt. My mind buzzed. Just because I could get the flights for free, how could I get the accommodations? *Who was I to even think I could do something like this? Wasn't it selfish? Wasn't it crazy?* I'd never taken a single vacation growing up. *This isn't what regular people do!* I told myself.

In that moment I made a split-second decision: I got the tickets. I had no idea how I'd make the trip work, I didn't even know if I could get the time off. I just *did it.* I saw the opportunity, I knew it wasn't a random coincidence, and I took the leap of faith.

I know it might sound crazy, but this is how manifesting works. It almost *always* requires you to silence the doubt and act on an opportunity.

That August, Kanen and I sat together on the sand watching the sunset over the ocean in Maui. I'd found an affordable little cottage room to rent and everything had seemed to magically come together perfectly. We'd had a long and happy day. Our faces were sunburned, our legs sore from our surfing lessons that morning, and our hearts were bursting with the excitement that only comes from experiencing something new and magical together. We sipped the water from our coconuts and chatted excitedly about what the next few days would bring, and I squeezed him tight.

I would build my life around that feeling of joy.

That was the moment I realized *why* it's the *moments* and *experiences* that matter. I knew right then that from then on I would build my life around that feeling of joy, those moments of connection, love, and happiness.

I went back to the office renewed, knowing I could work hard to make anything happen. I realized that living experiences like that is what mattered most to me and I understood they'd require faith and tolerance for taking risks. I promised myself that I'd live my life with this guiding principle and it has never let me down.

Creating Your #LiveList

Everything you've done up to this point has prepared you for *this*! It's the ultimate exercise to help you reveal and push past your blocks to manifesting. Are you ready? Let's play a little game of pretend.

Imagine that I've just handed you a $5 million check. Hold up, there's a catch! (*I know, right? There's always a catch with an imaginary free $5 million!*) This check comes with two strings:

1. You must use it all within your lifetime.

2. You can't buy material things with it.

Yep! That means there will be no buying of mansions, no ordering custom-made Ferraris, no paying off mortgages, and no investing in retirement plans.

So if you can't buy *things* with this money, what can you do with it? Here's what you can spend this money on: *doing* things. What would you *do* with this money that you could never do in your current life? This money is *only* to be spent on paying for *experiences*. It's for LIVING YOUR DREAM LIFE, not BUYING your dream life.

Think of it as the "play hard" part of the "work hard, play hard" equation. This is the stuff everyone dreams of *doing*! These are the things we think only the Kardashians can do, but no, I want you to imagine *yourself* doing those amazing things!

Your #LiveList allows you to create a life based on what makes you truly, blissfully happy. It turns conventional thinking on its head and measures success by the quality of LIFE you are living and the experiences you have.

Now I can hear the skeptic in you (or the Thinkers) say, "But Sarah, you didn't actually give me five million dollars!" To which I respond, "You must first be able to see it in your mind before you can live it in real life." If you can't "see it" in a fictional exercise, how could you ever manifest it in reality?

Stop stressing! The hardest part is just allowing yourself to imagine it in a "fake" scenario. If you are able to do that (and I know you are), then the magic has already begun. Those dreams have already been released into the Universe and they are starting their journey of finding their way back to you.

homework

Write down twenty-five *once-in-a-lifetime* moments/experiences you want to live in your lifetime. Don't filter them. Don't judge or question them. Just write them down. By now you've done enough work that this exercise should be a blast for Dreamers! Thinkers, you will see some ugly old voices in your head try and rear up, but you have the tools now to push past them to get this good work done! Remember that in this scenario I've given you five million imaginary dollars to spend on EXPERIENCES, NOT THINGS.

Let these questions help prompt your imagination to start roaming unchecked:

- What have I always wanted to *do*?

- Where have I always dreamed of going? What places would I love to visit? What would I do there? What time of year would I go? Who would I go with?

- What's the scariest thing I've ever wanted to try? Examples: sky-dive, bungie jump, be on TV, speak to a large crowd.

- If I could live anywhere in the world where would I live? If I could have a second home where would it be and what would I DO there? (This isn't about buying that home; it's about what LIFE would you have when you're in it.)

- What *big moment* have I always dreamed of living? Examples: signing a book you wrote at a book launch, crossing a marathon finish line, accepting an award.

- What would I do if I won the lottery? (Actual things you would *do*; this will further help you to get rid of money as a block.) Examples: throw a black-tie party for all my friends on a yacht, take my entire family on a European vacation, take my kids and their friends to Disneyland.

- What would I eat? Where would I eat it?

- Who would I meet?

I hate to burst your bubble, but this isn't about being an overnight millionaire. It's about living these experiences, long before you can "afford" them. That's what manifesting is: it's the ability to draw something into your life in a way that seems magical, unexpected, and accessible, regardless of your financial situation.

So silence the critic and allow your mind to just entertain the thought *What if? What if* I'm telling the truth? (I am by the way.) *What if* this could work for you too? (It can by the way.) But you've got to do your part, and right now that part is to start imagining your new life.

This is how it all begins.

When you write it down on paper, you are setting those dreams free. You are giving them a chance, an opportunity to find their way back to you. I think of them as little homing pigeons; you set them free, and eventually they come back. That's what you are doing here: racking your brain and getting creative and writing down all your wildest dreams.

See, most people wait their whole lives to live just a handful of big once-in-a-lifetime moments. We are taught to believe that those moments are only for retirement. Or only for the ultra-wealthy. Or only as a reward for some major accomplishment. Or only if you win the lottery. Surely those types of moments couldn't possibly be made for you and me, *right?* But they ARE! They really are. I have lived more than one hundred of those insane, pinch-me kinda moments since learning how to manifest in 2010. The rush of pure joy that fills every fiber of your being when you're living them is crazy! I want you to know what that feels like. I want you to create and LIVE that kind of magical life.

Before you get started there are a few rules:

1. **Don't put goals on this list.** Goals are not allowed! Examples of goals: pay off debt, buy a house, get a new car, become a

bestselling author, start a business or nonprofit, and so on. Those are all goals and do not belong on this list.

2. **Don't be vague.** Example: "I want to help people." Or "To be rich." Or "To be a good parent." All of these are not appropriate for this list.

3. **DO think of moments, experiences, things you want to do or try,** either by yourself or with loved ones. (Hint: It should be something you could take a photo of you *doing*.)

Summary

In this chapter you learned the importance of valuing experiences over material things. This concept is at the heart of what makes #FutureBoards work. You also learned why it's so important to build your life around experiences, because:

● They teach you how to create a life centered around happiness and joy.

● They teach you how to attach emotional "feeling" to visualization.

● They allow you to dream big without the normal hang-ups.

You've just completed my all-time favorite exercise, the #LiveList! It's the one that should really help you transform your thinking. By now, you've started to see all the possibilities that your life holds and begun getting excited for the day when these experiences show up in your life.

Everything you wrote on your #LiveList may also find its way onto your #FutureBoard in Part Two, so start thinking of each experience in visual image terms.

07: ANSWERING THE MILLION-DOLLAR QUESTION

This chapter will help you uncover the answers to the million-dollar question: *What do you want in your future life?* It seems easy enough, but trust me, this is one of the hardest questions I've posed so far. Many people really struggle with identifying what they want, so this chapter will be extremely important *for everyone*. Knowing what you want is the only way you'll ever get it. In this chapter, I'll walk you through how to answer this all-important question as it relates to the five core areas of your life.

Before you can start making your #FutureBoard, you must first have a clearly defined vision of your future life. #FutureBoards are created with *intention* to clearly depict your ideal future life and that's a main reason why they work so well, but in order to do that, you need to begin identifying what your future "dream life" looks like.

Creating Your New Future Life

Now that you've given yourself permission to dream HUGE by writing out your #LiveList and including items that pushed the barriers of your box, you can begin to answer the million-dollar question...

What do I want in my future life?

It's a broad question, I know, so I'm going to help you break it down to help you discover your own personal answers as they relate to the five core areas of your life.

Let go of what currently *is* and imagine entirely new realms of possibilities—ones you've probably never allowed yourself to consider.

Imagine.

Fantasize.

Daydream.

Ponder this: if you were the person you dream of being, living the life you dream of living... *Who would you be and what would your life look and feel like?*

In order to manifest anything, you need to first identify it as your heart's desire and then see it clearly in your mind.

Shift Your Focus

Begin by transferring your daily (hourly) focus from your current reality to this new imaginary future life. The more time you spend focusing on your future life, the more it will become part of you, creating desire, determination, belief, and hope. These elements help transition a thought into a vision, a vision into action, and action into reality.

Having a clear dream for your future life allows you to move forward with purpose and excitement rather than spending your days distraught about your present circumstances. If there's one thing I know without a shred of doubt, it's that what you focus on becomes your future. This means that focusing on the negatives in your current life is sabotaging your future success, ensuring that your life will never change or move forward in a positive direction. It's the most dangerous thing you can do and must be avoided at all costs.

Each time you imagine the details of your future life, take note of how it makes you feel. In the beginning, you might not feel much; it may seem forced or devoid of any emotional attachment. But push through and keep forcing yourself to slip into this fantasy on a daily (or hourly) basis. The more you do, the more attachment will grow. Our brains are pretty cool little computers; they believe whatever programing we feed them. Brains can't tell the difference between the truth or a lie when the lie is constantly repeated. So lie your ass off! Tell yourself this new lie and over time it will become your truth.

Need a little help putting it all together? Try this: Think of yourself as a film director. In his mind he sees the many parts of a movie before it all comes together on the big screen. He first visualizes what a scene will look like, then he takes the necessary action to put it together. All the while his mind is filming out other scenes and building them in much the same way.

This is how your future life begins to take shape in your mind. Start to imagine what a day in your new life would be like.

Clarity Is the Key to Manifesting

Be specific about your new life. See it in your mind. Let it grow. Let it inspire and motivate you. Now do that in all the areas of your life that need upgrading. Over time you will start to actually *feel* your future life and visualize those moments with such clarity and frequency that it will feel like just a matter of time. Allow these dreams to become part of you. The more you do this, the more you'll begin manifesting them in real life.

Remember that manifesting your dreams doesn't always follow your timeline. It's not bound by money. Not boxed in by the reality of your past or present. It doesn't adhere to "logic" or "rules." It has no limits. So *go crazy!* Stop limiting your life, your success, and your potential. Start seeing your "what ifs" as what is possible, instead of what's not. Give your dreams a chance to become your reality.

Personal Example

On September 21, 2011, I posted this on my blog: *Thoughts. Stories. Life.*

It's 2016: I am forty-one, Kanen is thirteen, and the girls (my twins) are nine years old.

I'm standing on the balcony of a villa in Tuscany, overlooking the Italian countryside. Vineyards stretch out over the rolling hills for as far as the eye can see! It's a warm summer evening, lavender drifting through the air.

I take a slow sip from my glass of wine, inhale the bouquet, let my nose do a little dance savoring the flavors as I swirl the liquid around my mouth.

There's a tall, gorgeous man walking toward me with an open bottle of Barbaresco. He graciously tops off my glass, leans in to kiss my forehead, and rests his hand on the small of my back. We lean against the brick balustrade and take in a long, relaxing, happy breath. I smile watching the girls play in the vineyard. They are kicking a soccer ball, trying to score goals against their strong, tall older brother. A few of the neighbor kids are playing too, working up a sweat, shouting soccer plays in Italian.

"My children are in Italy!" I think. They're laughing and saying things like "Ciao" and "Bella."

I've found my bliss. The kind of happiness that glows on the inside, and never stops manifesting itself on the outside. The kind that brings its best friend, joy, along for the ride. I'm brimming with a sense of peaceful calmness, a sensation I've rarely known.

I'm not worried or stressed. My brain is not overwhelmed with thoughts of bills, because money is no longer an issue. There are no schedules, or emails, text messages, Facebook, *or phones.*

Nothing but the joy of this moment occupies my thoughts.

Nothing but the joy of this moment occupies my thoughts. I don't have to work a nine-to-five job anymore. This is my reward for a lifetime of pain, suffering, struggle, and hustle.

Time does not expire here.

We play, we eat amazing food, we cook. We shop in the open-air markets. We drink wine and sip espresso.

The kids use their Italian to order dinner at dimly lit restaurants, where large Italian grandmothers bring us plates of meaty pasta. We eat fresh seafood that leathery old fishermen bring off their aging fishing boats. We dip warm freshly baked bread in cold-pressed olive oil.

We drive to the Riviera in a sports car, the girls and I with scarfs around our hair like 1940s movie stars. We stay in brightly colored stucco hotels overlooking the cliffs with the mist of the sea in the air. I'm drinking chilled champagne, the kids sipping on Italian sodas. We take the train, go to museums, and sing hymns in ancient cathedrals.

Our minds expand, our knowledge grows.

I feel beautiful. Perhaps for the first time in my life. I am fit and confident, the result of completing my first (and only) marathon.

In quiet moments I write. One day I'll hold in these hands a book I wrote.

This is all the heaven I need.

This is what I hustle for. This is my dream, and one day it will be my reality.

On October 3, 2016, the kids and I landed in Venice for a three-week, life-changing adventure through Italy. We stayed in a villa in Tuscany that overlooked olive orchards (not vineyards, but close enough!). The kids used their limited Italian to order at candlelit restaurants. A local Italian woman, who spoke little English, gave us a four-hour cooking class in Tuscany. We drove a tiny Fiat (not a sports car, but hey I'm not picky) to the Mediterranean. We hiked down the steep cliffs to see the colored houses clinging to the cliffside in Cinque Terre.

I had run that marathon the year before. I held a book that I wrote in my hands. I DO work for myself and own my time. I was forty-one. It was five years and twelve days after I wrote that post.

It was the realization of a dream I'd clung to for more than twenty years. The crazy part of this story? I had totally forgotten about this post and didn't even come across it again until months after returning from Italy. *That* is the power of this manifestation method! That's what dreams are capable of.

homework

Imagine yourself five years in the future. You are living your dream life! Every area of your life is blessed, goals have been reached, fortunes made, you feel amazing, you're surrounded by amazing people, and you do amazing things. So then, who are you? And what does this life look like?

To help get your creative juices flowing write the responses to these questions in your journal. In this new life:

- **What does your average day look and feel like?** Get as detailed in this description as you possibly can. Write out your day from getting out of bed in the morning to falling asleep at night. What is so fabulous about it? Remember this is a life you are about to start working hard to manifest so it's gotta be the bee's knees! Why do you love it so much? Is it where you live? Describe your dream home. What do the kitchen and yard look like? How do they make you feel to be in them? Can you feel your family in those spaces, laughing and loving life? What kind of car do you drive? Where do you go on vacation?

- **What are you doing for work?** Since this is your dream future life, you're in your dream job. What is it? Where do you go to work every day? What does your workspace look like? Who works with you? Describe your dream work environment in vivid detail down to the office, the building, the people, how much you work each day, how much you get paid. All of it.

- **Who is in your life?** Are you married? Do you have kids? What do they do? Describe your relationships as you dream them to be, in their best form. Think about who would be in your new life that might not be in your current one. Do you have mentors? Friends?

- **What do you do for fun?** How do you unwind and relax? What do you do to feel most alive and exhilarated? What brings you joy on a daily basis? Gardening? Cooking? Dancing? Yoga? Art? Photography? What is it for you?

- **How do you spend your money?** In this awesome new life that you're creating, money won't be an issue, so in that case, how do you spend it? What does wealth and abundance look like to you? Does it mean a lake house or a beach house in addition to your dream house? Does it mean a boat or a sports car? Or does it mean luxury treatments for yourself like spa getaways or international first-class travel? This will be different for everyone, so what does wealth LOOK like to you and FOR you?

Write it all out. Describe it with as much detail as you possibly can. Go crazy! Remember you can manifest only what you can identify, so it's your job in this exercise to identify it all.

Now how does it feel to know what you want?! You've answered the million-dollar question! How do you feel looking at your future life on paper? A life that you've custom-built just for you?! If you're anything like me, it feels AHHHMAZING!

Tips for Thinkers

How you doing? I know this is a lot to take in, I'm asking a lot of you here. It requires a little *blind faith* and I get that might not be your thing. But you did *awesome*! I'm so proud of you for doing this work.

I know it's not easy. I know you had to silence a lot of critical internal voices to get this assignment done, and I just want you to know that I'm giving you a giant hug for being such a badass and doing it!

You are brave. You are strong. You are DOING THIS!

One step closer baby!

Tips for Dreamers

Are you about to come out of your skin with excitement or what?! This is one of my all-time favorite exercises and one I redo every year. It gets me so amped, because I can totally see and feel my new life!

You've taken a HUGE step to get this thing off the ground and I'm just so stinkin' proud of you!

P.S. This isn't like all the other times you've had a big dream and then lost steam. This time you TOOK ACTION; you did this homework and by doing it you've put the Universe into action on your behalf. It's already at work (as you read this) to start lining up this life and all these amazing experiences for you. How cool is that? It's already on its way. It is in process!

Manifesting Happens in Stages

I've learned through experience that manifesting comes in stages. Reading that blog post sent chills through my entire body because so much of it had materialized on that trip without conscious planning (which is insane!). But still, there are a few details that haven't materialized yet. For instance, there is no tall, dark, and handsome Italian stallion by my side! However, because manifesting happens when the timing is in our best interest, I fully expect to one day watch the sunset at *my* Italian villa with the love of my life beside me. Maybe it will be my grandkids who are playing soccer instead of my kids, but either way… that moment is still in process!

Summary

Oh, boy! You've learned a lot in Part One already haven't you? By now your journal should be like a bestie, holding all your dreams, plans, and hopes for the future.

I know it can be frustrating at first, not immediately starting off making your physical #FutureBoard, but I hope by now you understand why the work you did in Part One was critical to laying the foundation before the board can be made.

The foundational work you've just completed is the meat to all of this. It's what answers the toughest questions about your life: how it is now, why it's that way, and how to change your results moving forward. And finally, in this last chapter in Part One you answered the all-important question: *What do I want?*

I am so proud of you! You did it. The hardest part of this process is over and now the fun begins! Let's make a #FutureBoard!

DURING

Making Your #FutureBoard

Now the fun begins, it's time to make your #FutureBoard!

Part Two of this book has only two chapters, because I teach this process in two phases. Step 1 is all about how to find the right pictures and create an online version of your board. In this phase, you'll learn how to create boards for your five core categories, determine what you want in each, and find the right pictures to represent those desires.

I'll walk you through how I create these boards so you can learn to constantly surround yourself with different visuals of your dreams. This process allows your visualization and emotional attachment skills to grow and expand, constantly pushing the boundaries on your dreams. This process also teaches you how to use your online boards to keep you focused and motivated on the go, using an app as a positive, proactive way to spend your time online.

Step 2 to creating your physical #FutureBoard is physically assembling it. I walk you through this process in an easy, step-by-step guide. Are you ready to make your personal manifesting masterpiece? Let's get started!

08: YOUR BOARD BEGINS ONLINE

This chapter covers how to make your online #Future-Board and find the right pictures to represent all your dreams and future life. These are the photos you'll use in Step 2, when you make your physical board.

Identifying the Five Core Areas

You are about to learn my two biggest secrets to creating a #Future-Board that *works*! This is my secret sauce. It's the reason my boards manifest so accurately and quickly and it's the biggest difference between a #FutureBoard and a standard "vision board."

- #FutureBoards are holistic, identifying what you want in the **five core areas** of your life with specificity.

- They are made with the RIGHT pictures.

Because manifesting is all about the Universe bringing you more of what you put out, you want the life you are creating to be based in happiness. The last thing you want is to create a life that is financially successful, but lonely and unfulfilled. No thank you! I want the life you're creating to grow in happiness and abundance with each level of success for the rest of your life.

You started this process in your last homework assignment, but now it's time to break these five categories into clear areas of focus, so you can begin finding the photos for your board in each area.

The Five Core Areas Are:

1. Relationships

2. Career and Ambitions

3. Mind and Body

4. Passions and Joy

5. Wealth and Abundance

Pictures Matter

Finding the *right* photographs, ones that match the vision you've created of your future life, makes all the difference in the world. This is why random magazine pictures just won't do. The chances of finding pictures that represent your perfect relationships, career, what wealth means to you, or anything else, in this month's issue of any magazine, are pretty slim. Random pictures don't stimulate manifesting power because they aren't emotionally attached to your personal vision and dreams. The photos *must* match the images that already exist in your mind.

Personally, I find most of my pictures on *Pinterest*, but you can also discover great photos using *Google Images*, blogs, and other photography-centric websites. The thing I like about *Pinterest* in particular is it's not social media. It's a search engine with an enormous library of beautiful photography. I've found that most people who attend my workshops or coaching programs don't know how to use it for this purpose, thought it was only for crafting and DIY projects, or don't use it at all. If that's you, I've provided the following step-by-step guide on how I use it to create my online boards, find my photos, and speed up manifesting.

Pro tip: Need a visual example? Take a look at my boards on *Pinterest* to see examples of how I've created each one, what the sections inside the boards look like, and examples of photos I Pin, to demonstrate a visual of the LIFE I'm building in each board. It will really help you connect all the dots with this exercise. You can find me on *Pinterest* as Sarah Centrella.

While you're there, take a look at my "REALITY Board." This board hosts my photographic proof of all the moments, things, and experiences I've manifested since 2010.

One section has side-by-side examples showing a photo on my #Future-Board and a photo of my manifestation, the story and timeline of each one will be in the caption. There's also a board with all the Pins I've manifested directly from my *Pinterest* board, over one hundred! There really is magic in doing both the online version and the physical board.

How to Find the Right Pictures

As I mentioned, there are many online sites you can visit to find the pictures for your #FutureBoard. Because I personally use *Pinterest* I will use that app for tutorial purposes, but remember you should feel free to use any website or app you desire. Here's how to get started:

Using the Pinterest App

- **Click on the P icon** in the lower left-hand corner to pull up your "feed." Note: The feed is made up of Pins from people you follow and also Pins that *Pinterest*'s algorithms have selected as ones you might like based on what you've recently Pinned. This is a great feature as it will continually show you other versions of things you've Pinned that might help make your vision and dream even more clear and more exciting. If something in this feed looks awesome to you, be sure to Pin it to your appropriate boards.

- **From your feed go to the "search" box at the top of the app.** Important: Enter search terms for the picture you want *Pinterest* to find and *always* be sure to add the word *photography* at the end. This tip is everything! When you add the word *photography* to your search it will filter out all the junk and give you beautiful pictures, which is what you want. Now, not all search terms are created equal, so play around with it until the type of photos you want to see begin pulling up.

- **Once you find a picture you *love*, tap it.** When you do, the photo will enlarge and in the bottom right corner you'll see a small white square. This is an awesome feature because it allows you to tell *Pinterest* to go find you more pictures that look similar to the one you've selected. Tap the square and use the crop tool to select which part of the photo you'd like to see more examples of. When you do this, several new photos should pop up that look pretty similar giving you more options.

- **Be sure to pick pictures that really speak to you.** Find the ones that instantly get that movie playing in your head. Photos that help you see the images that started as a thought in your mind come to life before your eyes.

- **Once you've found that perfect picture, Pin it to the appropriate virtual board.** One of the reasons I love using *Pinterest* is that not only can I find beautiful pictures; I can also put them in my virtual boards. This provides several additional benefits that will speed up the manifesting process.

First, I can add photos to those boards the way most people scroll *Facebook* or *Instagram* mindlessly, as a "time-out" escape. But unlike those social platforms, my time on *Pinterest* is actually productive. Every time I search for a photo in one of my core categories, my mind is exposed to new visuals of that dream, which helps expand and clarify my vision. It helps me "see" and "feel" my future life in a fresh way. It enables me to push the boundaries of my box, expanding my dreams by showing me visual variations of that dream I may not have previously considered. Because of this, I try to spend any downtime adding to my boards.

Second, it's a great way to get out of a temporary "funk." If I've had a hard day, lost a deal in my business, or faced a setback, I can spend thirty minutes Pinning pictures of a woman traveling through Europe, and BOOM! I'm back! It refocuses me and helps me get a fresh glimpse of the big picture that I'm always hustling for. It's the perfect, quick shot of motivation in the palm of my hand!

Relationships

This category is all about the people who will ideally surround you in this new life. For example:

- If you're not married, but you want to be, you'll look for pictures of a couple doing things you imagine doing with the love of your life. You'll also want to find images that represent marriage and/or a wedding.

- If you want a romantic relationship, find photos of a couple inter-acting, showing love and doing things together. Look for images that show them doing things you love doing, and displaying emotions that are important to you (laughter, joy, smiles, chivalry, cooking, camping, sports, and so on).

- If you want kids, do the same thing. Find photos of how you see your family evolving, what types of things you'd do together, maybe even what their bedrooms would look like. If you have kids already, find photos of things you want to do with them. What types of memories do you want them to have about their childhood?

- If you want more friends in your life, find photos of groups of people doing things together: barbecuing, eating dinner, camping, or whatever you like doing with friends.

● If you want mentors or business partners in your life, find photos of people helping each other, talking together, having lunch, or working together.

If you already have some or all of those relationships in your life currently, think about how you can take them to the next level. If you're married, find pictures that show a couple doing things that are lacking in your relationship (time spent together having fun, vacations, and so on), or showing emotions you want to experience more often. If you want more intimacy, search for photos of couples laughing, holding hands, hugging each other, kissing.

Try to get creative on what things you can *do* with the people in your life that will enrich your life. Can you travel with your kids? Can you cook with your significant other? Can you do a monthly girls' night? What types of things would you do? Would you love to do a girls' trip? Where would you go?

All of these ideas are how you begin to search for the pictures that will visually show you what your life is going to look and feel like.

Build Your Relationship Board

Again, for purposes of this example I'll be using the Pinterest app, but feel free to use your preferred method.

1 Touch the plus (+) icon in the top right corner to create a new board.

2 Select "Board."

3 Name your board "Relationships." Note: You can choose to keep your board secret if you wish, but I say let the world know; it's part of the process of manifesting and owning your dreams! Then select "Create." Now you have a blank board where all your photos of healthy, happy relationships will go.

4 Add sections. Once you've created your "relationships" board, click on it. It will be empty, but you'll see "Add section." Sections are awesome! They are like smaller buckets within a bucket and they help you organize your five key boards in a way that will help you define what you want in several specific areas within a given topic.

SAMPLE BOARD

My "relationships" board has five sections within it. These sections help me identify what I *want* various relationships in my life to look and feel like in their ideal state.

My sections include:

Family. This section contains photos of things I'd like to *do* with my children and how I see our family living and enjoying life. Sample search: family cooking together photography.

Girlfriends. These are photos of things I'd like to do with my friends, how I visualize those relationships when they are at their *ideal* state. For instance, if I have just a few close friends and I'd like a bigger friend crew, I'd find pictures of lots of girls hanging out and doing fun things together. Sample search: women front row at fashion show photography.

Love. This board is for manifesting romantic love. It's how I "see" love and what a healthy, loving, caring, and fun relationship "looks" like to me. Sample search: couple laughing sharing tender moment photography.

Future husband. This board has photos of my dream dude. The one that will manifest once my kids go off to college and I move to Italy! Sample search: George Clooney in Italy photography!

Dream wedding. It's pretty beautiful, y'all should go check it out!

People often ask me if they should cut out photos of their (and/or their loved ones) faces and glue them over the faces of people in the photos they've found online. The answer is no. You don't need to go to that extreme; it's much more important that the photos you find are ones where you can "see yourself" as the person in the photo. You can imagine that it's you and that's enough.

Another common question is "Can I add a photo of a former love on my board and manifest them coming back into my life?" Over the years I've gotten so many messages from people who want to know how they manifest the person they love who's no longer in their life—sometimes it's an ex, sometimes it's unrequited love. In either case, I always say no.

The truth is, if that relationship was the right one for you, you'd be with that person right now. The Universe can see your future in a way that you cannot. If you've taken the time to truthfully identify what you want in the "relationship" category of your new life, then it knows your heart's desire. Chances are, if you're really honest with yourself, that past love was not everything you want. That's not always easy to see when you're going through it; I know this firsthand. But trust the process and trust the Universe to have your back. It won't let you down.

It might take some time before you are ready to receive the right person into your life and the Universe knows this too. It's preparing you. It's preparing them. It's preparing the planets to align when the time is right, probably when you're least expecting it. Trust that it knows what's in your best interest and that letting go of the person you're clinging to is necessary in order to manifest the one who is meant for you.

Career and Ambitions

For many people (especially Thinkers) this area is already fairly well-defined. That's because many of us were brought up to focus on setting and achieving career ambitions. We are conditioned from a young age to think of our life in terms of measurable goals, so this might come easy for you. If that's the case, you can still push your dreams to a whole new level. You don't want your life to be stagnant in any area, career included, so what's the next level of success for you? For example:

- If you own a business, what is your ultimate long-term goal with that business? What would "unparalleled success" look like if your business exploded? Would you franchise it? Would you sell it? Would you open multiple offices? Would you get a bigger office? What's the biggest version of success you could imagine? Find pictures that *show* what this looks like.

- If you are in a career where advancement is a possibility, what's the highest level you'd like to reach in the company (or another company)? What's that title? What would your average day look like if you were in that role?

- If you work for a company or organization and you want to eventually work for yourself or become a digital nomad, what would that look like?

Of course, not everyone knows what their "dream" job is and that's okay too. This process will help you uncover that answer too.

If your career path is unclear, you can begin uncovering it by defining your "dream" work environment. Even though you don't yet know *what* you'd be doing in this "dream career," you can identify if you'd like to be working from home, a beach, or in a beautiful office in your future life.

Tips for Dreamers

If you don't know what your dream career is yet, don't stress. Often Dreamers struggle "finding their career path" and/or sticking to it.

In my experience Dreamers tend to change jobs more regularly than Thinkers, because they are easily distracted by the next shiny object. If you can relate, don't beat yourself up. It just means you haven't yet tapped into your true passion.

Without passion we are easily distracted and discouraged when the going gets tough or the newness wears off. It's okay to not know what your exact dream career is at this stage. It's even okay to not know what you're passionate about.

If you have done all the homework, and dug deep on each assignment, those answers will find you soon enough.

Be open to new opportunities and aware of what begins to show up in your life. Chances are it's your purpose (or "calling") rising to the surface.

Or maybe you'd like to lead a team, or be surrounded by talented coworkers or employees. You can articulate if you'd rather have the freedom and flexibility to work from anywhere in the world, if you'd like to regularly travel, or if you'd rather work independently. You can pick out all these elements right now!

When you begin answering these questions you can get creative and start to see their answers visually in your mind. Once you do, then you can search for the pictures to match.

Getting clarity on what that working environment feels like, how you'll feel in it, and what your day might consist of sets manifesting energy in motion. Be sure to remain open and ready to act when new opportunities present themselves, because your "dream job" may very well be something you've never previously considered.

Personal Example

My calling found me. I was all set to be a corporate boss chick, making my six-figure salary, earning my commissions, taking my business trips, and living a life that was already beyond my wildest dreams, when my true passion/purpose/calling bubbled to the surface.

If you had asked me in 2010 if I would be a bestselling author, an international motivational speaker, a master life coach working with NBA and NFL athletes, and coaching people around the world on how to live their dreams, I would have broken out in hysterical laughter! "Who, *me*?" I'd have responded, mouth agape.

But after a few years I began imagining a different working environment, one that was *not* corporate. I wanted the freedom to travel the world with my kids, to be waiting for them when they got home from school, to work when and how I wanted. I wanted out of the pressure of a nine-to-five job.

And somewhere along the way I began listening to my gut, my heart, and my intuition. I began writing online, first just for my own sanity. Slowly, I started responding when people asked for advice. When my advice worked, and demand grew, eventually I began coaching. Then somehow I wrote a book. I began speaking and teaching people all over the world how to do what I have done. I did *all of that* while holding down a full-time corporate job. I was still unsure, not ready to take the leap of faith and trust what had become, over time, my true passion and purpose.

It was the Universe that stepped in and eventually forced my hand. I knew the time had come for me to be all in for my new career. I also knew that in order to do that, I'd have to let go of a secure paycheck. As a single mom, that was terrifying.

I began listening to my gut, my heart, and my intuition.

I had so many doubts, so many fears, just like anyone would in that situation. But in my heart of hearts I knew it was time for me to make the move. When I was unexpectedly fired from my corporate job in February of 2017, I knew. It was time. I would *never* work for anyone else again.

Ambitions

Ambitions represent achievements you'd like to accomplish in your lifetime. Some examples of these are: run a marathon, win an award, write a book, climb some huge mountain, see every continent, be written about in some famous magazine, earn a degree…you get the idea. When you're searching for these photos, be sure to find ones with either a man or woman (depending on how you identify) in that moment.

Personal Example

I had a picture of a woman crossing a marathon finish line and a 26.2 sticker on my #FutureBoards from 2009–2013.

Which brings me to the *worst* thing I've ever manifested! In October of 2014 I crossed the finish line of the Portland Marathon, *after seven-plus hours of running*! Yes, you read that right…SEVEN grueling, wretched hours. By the time I finally finished, they'd already removed the finish line. There were no fans, no camera crews—hell, there wasn't even any more tape blocking off the road! But there were my three babies, holding signs that read "You did it, Mama!" and "We believe in you!" And that was enough.

In truth, I did it to *prove* to myself that this method you're learning can work on something as tangible (and awful) as a nonrunner completing a marathon. And it did.

Build Your Career and Ambitions Board

For the purposes of this example I'll be using the Pinterest app, but feel free to use your preferred method for building your board.

1 **As in your previous board, first touch the plus (+) icon in the top right corner to create a new board.** And then select "Board."

2 **Name your board "Career and Ambitions."** Then select "Create."

3 **Add sections.** Here's where you will want to break out the various sections of your career and life ambitions into separate sections.

SAMPLE BOARD

My "career" board has several sections within it that represent the various parts of my dream career. My sections include:

Speaking. This section contains photos of women giving speeches to stadiums, pictures of a microphone, and of me giving speeches. Sample search: woman public speaking photography.

TV dreams. These are photos representing my dream to have a talk show one day. Sample search: Oprah at *The Oprah Winfrey Show* photography.

Books. This board shows my dreams around being a repeat bestselling author. Sample search: woman writing photography.

Retreats. This board has photos of the vibe I want to create at future retreats both in the US and internationally. Sample search: woman at wellness retreat photography.

Office space. This board shows the various ways I see where I work. Both a beautiful home office, working from around the world, and having a beautiful physical office leading a powerful team. Sample search: woman laptop Paris photography.

Mind and Body

I believe that to build a truly happy life, you need to take care of your physical body and your mind. I am the first to admit that this has not always been easy for me. I've struggled with my weight on and off my whole life. That struggle has taught me that I am *not* happy when I'm not physically active or in good health. When I stop exercising, start eating crap, and generally get lazy I feel like shit! It doesn't matter how successful other parts of my life are in that moment, I will not be happy. I will feel guilt and shame. I'll hide in pictures. I'll dread pictures being taken of me. I'll dress sloppy because it's all that feels comfortable. I'll sabotage my success by turning down on-camera work because I don't want to see myself.

The same is true of my mind. If I'm not meditating on a regular basis, or going to yoga or writing, I will fall off the wagon. I'll begin allowing negative, destructive thoughts to throw a party in my untended mind and before I know it, everything seems to be falling apart.

Thankfully, I've gotten to know myself pretty well the past few years, and I know what I need to do to stay on track and feel my best. I know that every single day I have a choice to either keep doing what I know works and is good for me, or not.

I've had to make this a priority in my life, knowing that I won't reach the level of success I desire if I'm not taking care of myself. This board is a reminder to do that every day. It's a visual reminder of what that looks like.

If you are a person of faith, the "mind" category of this board is where you want to represent that. This is where you'll ask yourself what does faith look like for me? When I'm exercising my faith, what am I doing? Praying? Going to church? Doing a daily devotional? Being of service? Find pictures that show people doing those activities.

Creating Your Mind and Body Board

Here is how you would build your board using the Pinterest app.

1 As in your previous board, first touch the plus (+) icon in the top right corner to create a new board. And then select "Board."

2 Name your board "Mind and Body."

3 **Add sections.** Add a section for physical activity and one for how you take care of your mind (meditation, prayer, faith, reading, and so on).

SAMPLE BOARD

My "mind and body" board has three sections within it. These "show" me what being mentally and physically at my best looks like. My sections include:

Nutrition/healthy eating. This section contains photos of healthy food and recipes. Sample search: healthy clean eating photography.

Body/fitness. These photos show all the various ways I enjoy getting and staying physically fit. Yoga, boxing, running, barre3, and so on. It's important to search for pictures with either a man or woman (or however you identify) doing the activity. It's also important that you find photos of people who have the body type that you *want*. For instance, if I'm searching for photos of women running, I won't choose a photo of a skinny twenty-year-old blonde. I'm not blond. I'm not twenty. My goal is not to be skinny. Personally, I have a different body type that I'm aspiring to, so I want the picture to be as accurate as possible. Sample search: woman running on the beach photography.

Mind. This board shows pictures of how I recharge my mind: meditation, reading, quiet, nature, yoga. You might have things like: listening to podcasts (find a picture of man or woman with headphones on), praying, daily devotion, church, going for a walk. Sample search: woman meditating outside photography.

Passions and Joy

This is a tricky area of our life, because most of us are not conditioned to make passions, hobbies, and joy an important part of our life. We think they are a luxury; one we'll indulge when we have "extra time." But who ever has *that*?!

Passions and joy are *very* important, arguably a critical part of manifesting the life you want. Because they are one of the fastest ways for you to *feel* joy and happiness *right now*. It's important to infuse your present reality with as much happiness as possible because that *feeling* is what generates manifesting happiness in the future. A regular feeling of happiness enables you to make good decisions, ones that keep you aligned with that feeling. It also keeps you grateful for every manifestation along the way.

Passions and hobbies also serve another important purpose: they allow you to mentally check out or refresh in a positive way. When you are participating in an activity you love, it takes your mind off everything else. It relieves stress and clears your overtaxed brain. It's one of the few ways you can easily access these benefits in your hectic daily life. They bring your life balance, they help you appreciate what life is all about, and they give you an excuse to slow down and enjoy the journey.

Don't know what your passions are? Don't have hobbies? Think about things you loved to do as a kid. Did you ride horses? Play with animals? Grow a garden? Cook? Bake? Paint? Write? Draw? Travel? Dance? Craft? Build things? Fix things? Play sports? Swim? Sing? Play an instrument? Sew? Write? Ride bikes? Do photography? Run? Practice yoga? Hike?

All of those are great examples of hobbies and passions. They might not be "passions" right now, but give them a try. You might find they grow on you. Try several until you discover things you can do, easily and regularly, to inject joy into your life. Things that give you that sense of refresh.

Creating Your Passions and Joy Board

Here is how you would build your board using the Pinterest app.

1 **As in your previous board, first touch the plus (+) icon in the top right corner to create a new board.** And then select "Board."

2 **Name your board "Passions and Joy."**

3 **Add sections.** See the previous examples of hobbies to get ideas of what sections to create.

SAMPLE BOARD

My sections on my "passions and joy" board include:

Flowers. Flowers make me happy. I mean they not only bring a genuine smile to my face when I buy them, they make me *feel* joy and gratitude every time I look at them. So I buy fresh flowers for my house every single week. I love arranging them and growing them. Sample search: tulips flowers arrangement photography.

Photography. Photography is my biggest personal hobby. I have been taking pictures since I was in high school and in my twenties I took several photography classes in college and dreamed of being a professional. It's something I can do on *any* given day to bring joy into my life. Sample search: woman taking pictures photography.

Cooking. I love to cook, especially for my family. I'm always looking for new recipes and ways to involve my kids in the kitchen. It's something I do daily to feel grounded, happy, and blessed. Sample search: woman cooking with kids photography.

Travel. Travel is my absolute passion. It's my greatest wish to travel the world with my kids. It's such a passion in fact that I have several travel boards on *Pinterest*—it's expanded beyond just this board! Sample search: woman riding a camel in Dubai photography.

Wealth and Abundance

In my experience, this has been the hardest category for people to identify when it comes time to make their boards. Why? Because we are not conditioned to consider what having more money will actually mean to us. Instead we've been taught to believe that it's all about having a specific number in our bank account. How much money would it take for you to "be happy"? A few hundred thousand? A million? Ten million? The answer is, it doesn't matter.

People think that money is the ultimate motivator, but it's not. Why? Because if you've never had a lot of money, you can't understand what it would feel like to have it, or how it will change your life. If you've lived paycheck to paycheck most of your life, then money simply means "paying the bills." Even if you've lived comfortably, you can't really understand what true "wealth" would feel like.

I once had a boss call me into his office and ask me why the sales team was not motivated by a huge bonus opportunity he'd just offered. "I don't get it. Why isn't it *The Hunger Games* out there?" he asked. "Because it's just hypothetical money," I told him. "You can't offer a check bigger than anyone has ever seen and expect them to stay motivated. They immediately believe it must be unattainable, therefore why try?" They don't know what it would feel like to have that check in their bank. Also, most people translate money into *what debt can I pay with that?* And that's even less motivating!

"Offer an all-expense-paid family vacation to the winner," I suggested. He laughed. "Are you serious? It's a quarter of what the cash prize would be!" But it worked. The team was instantly motivated because it was something they could relate to. It meant something.

This is a perfect example of *why* I want you to get away from thinking about money as a dollar amount and start thinking about how it will change your quality of life. Where you'll live, what car you'll drive, where and how you'll vacation, who your friends will be. Name it all. Claim it all. Be specific! What does "wealth" and "abundance" mean to you?

Another reason we stay away from specific dollar amounts is that your goal could be to *have a million dollars*. Ever hear the phrase "be careful what you wish for"? If your wish was $1 million you could manifest it, but you could also manifest owing $1.5 million! Or you could cap yourself out at $1 million. We don't want either of those scenarios! We want to create and imagine a limitless *lifestyle* and a happy abundant *life*.

We want to create and imagine a limitless lifestyle and a happy abundant life.

These images will become much more motivating as you work toward your dreams than a dollar amount could ever be! Whenever I'm frustrated about my dreams not happening at "Sarah speed," I look at my board and remind myself that *this* is the life I am hustling for. It's a life and a lifestyle I could have never attained in the corporate world, and it motivates me to never give up on my hustle or my dreams.

This is the one board where you put photos of material things. Because they show you what money means to *you*.

Creating Your Wealth and Abundance Board

Here is how you would build your board using the Pinterest app.

1 **As in your previous board, first touch the plus (+) icon in the top right corner to create a new board.** And then select "Board."

2 **Name your board "Wealth and Abundance."**

3 **Add sections.** If you were endlessly wealthy how would you spend your money? A dream home? Luxury? Travel? Designer duds? Vacation houses?

SAMPLE BOARD

The sections on my "wealth and abundance" board include:

Luxury lifestyle. This section has images of the lifestyle I am creating. This is what wealth "looks" like to *me*. Remember wealth is subjective and means something different for everyone. But make sure that you're not selling yourself short here either. This board has pictures of dream jewelry, speedboats, shopping, spa days, and anything else that I imagine when I think of the term "money is no object." Sample search: woman dripping in diamonds photography.

Dream cars. This board holds pictures of various dream cars, beautiful photography where I can imagine myself behind the wheel. Sample search: vintage Land Rover photography.

Jet-setter. To me the ultimate symbol of wealth is a private jet. So this board has lots of those! Plus, yachts. Sample search: woman flying on private jet photography.

Dream home. I actually have a full separate board for my dream home that includes every room in the home. A city version, a country version, a lake/beach version, a she shed, and the yard! I've got this one down! Sample search: dream home white exterior photography.

You're Not Done Yet!

Now that your five core boards are created I want you to make two additional boards. Title them:

1. "#LiveList"

2. "Master #FutureBoard"

Your #LiveList board will be filled with all the amazing photos to match the list from your earlier homework. You've already identified twenty-five once-in-a-lifetime moments, now it's time to find the pictures to match those moments (and more!). Go crazy! Pinning to this board is my go-to happy place—I have over five hundred Pins in this board. So if you need a little kick-start for your imagination, go check out mine.

Your Master #FutureBoard will be the place you Pin your absolute favorite pictures from each of your other boards.

Now it's time to fill each board with beautiful photos that will ignite your imagination, fuel and inspire your dreams, and give you excited butterflies! Allow yourself to really get into this exercise. It may take a little bit, but the longer you find and post pictures, the more you'll begin to let go and dream HUGE!

This isn't just a one-time thing. You will probably need to spend at least a week filling your boards. Just hop on your app when you have some time to kill throughout the day, or in the evening when it's quiet and peaceful. Find photos instead of scrolling social media. Post *all* the photos that excite you, dumping them into their appropriate boards and sections.

Pro tip: I often think of something specific to search for before I open my Pinterest app. For example: If I'm feeling down, I know that searching for international travel photography will cheer me up, and soon I'll be imagining the day when it's *me* taking those photos. If I'm worried or stressed financially, I'll Pin photos of "wealth" and "abundance" to help refocus my mind and draw those positive results into my life. When I'm a little lonely, it's photos of "relationships" and "love" that I focus on. Having something in mind really helps get the most from your searches.

Once those boards have *many* photo examples in each category and each section, then you can go through and put your favorites in your Master #FutureBoard. This board will eventually hold the photos for your physical #FutureBoard.

Now can you see your future life take shape? It's so exciting, *right?* Now do you see why you can't use magazines? Why a "vision board party" just ain't gonna cut it?! Is it all making sense?

This really is custom creating your life. It's so much more than just pictures.

No Quotes Allowed!

If you are a newbie to this, you might be tempted to fill your board with quotes. DON'T! This is a *visual* board. Its job is to stimulate your *visual* senses, which you need to kick your visualization skills into gear. That's a critical part of manifesting. Quotes do not accomplish this goal; they don't visually translate.

homework

Journal time! Answer these questions and write about how you are feeling right now.

- What excites you most about your new life?
- What area of your life, or what board/section gives you excited chills?
- What has this process taught you about yourself that you didn't previously know?
- Have you dreamed bigger than you did before?
- What do you want now that you never wanted before?
- Do you believe you will one day live it?

Stay away from putting words on your board as well. I have the words for each category on my board, but that's about it. Why? Because words are subjective, they mean different things to everyone. And frankly they are a cop-out! People gravitate to words and quotes when they can't (or don't know how to) identify what they want. Quotes and words are a way to avoid digging deep or pushing yourself. And that's not you! You've done all this work to get clarity and definition around your future, so don't chicken out now. Hunt for the picture, not the words.

Hunt for the picture, not the words.

If there's a word, or a quote that is *really* calling to you, ask yourself how you'd visually represent it in a photo.

For instance, take the word *believe*. Personally, it's one of my favorite words. But on a visual board what does that word mean? I want to dig deep enough within myself to get that answer. What does it look like when I *believe*? What do I *believe* in? What activity, or state, am I in when I *believe*?

For some *believe* might be a religious or faith-based word, one used to mean "believe in God." For me it means "I believe in myself, my dreams, my passion…" It might mean something totally different to you.

On my 2018 board, I demonstrated what "believe" means to me. It's a photo of a woman sitting crisscross-applesauce on a beach. She's meditating as the sun sets in front of her. Her palms are facing the sky; her eyes are closed. She's in a beautiful setting (somewhere I'd love to be). She's at peace. Her belief has been rewarded. She is receiving more faith and belief from the energy around her. She is strong on her own. That is what "believe" looks like to me, *right now*. When I look at the photo, I remind myself to keep believing. See what I mean?

Summary

How are you feeling now that you are starting to *see* your future life? This is such an exciting part of the process for me. It's the moment when you can finally start attaching actual visuals to each of your dreams, bringing them to life.

You've learned in this section how to create a life that is holistic and addresses your wants and desires in the five core areas of your life. Which are:

1. Relationships

2. Career and Ambitions

3. Mind and Body

4. Passions and Joy

5. Wealth and Abundance

These boards will remain evergreen. You'll add to them whenever you need a little inspiration or motivation.

You've also created two additional online boards:

1. Your #LiveList

2. Your Master #FutureBoard

You are now ready to print the photos in your Master #FutureBoard and create the physical masterpiece!

09: ASSEMBLING YOUR PHYSICAL #FUTUREBOARD

The moment you've been waiting for has arrived: it's time to make your physical #FutureBoard! Everything you've learned so far, every homework assignment you've completed, every hour you've spent finding the right pictures, has led to this. Are you ready? This is your step-by-step guide to creating the board that will hang on your wall.

Why You Need a Physical Board

I follow this same process every year when I create my new #Future-Board. It's a sacred ritual for me, something I look forward to and cherish. I believe the process of constructing your physical board is one that is extremely personal and shouldn't be rushed. That's why I always tell people who attend my workshops that they won't be completing their boards in class. I provide them with the tools, skills, and understanding of how to do it, but we don't ever finish them in a group setting.

One of the most frequent questions I'm asked is "Why do I need to make a physical board, if I already have an online one?" It's a great question and there are several reasons why it's such a critical part of the manifesting process:

1. **Because the Universe responds to *action*.** It takes time to make your physical board. It takes thought and planning. It takes action. The time you spend buying the right board, transferring the photos, then printing them, cutting them out, and arranging them, all of that is *action*. I believe the Universe waits to see if you are truly serious about your new intentions—it wants to see you put a little muscle behind your words. The physical act of making your board is that first tangible step toward your new life. It's not just thinking about it, or writing about it, or talking about it, it's *creating* it.

2. **The Universe responds to *energy*.** During each of the previously mentioned actions, you are *thinking* about your dreams and your future life—that is *energy*. You need this energy to bring you hope, excitement, clarity, vision, and belief as you make your board. And because the Universe responds to this optimistic

energy, it sets the wheels of manifesting in motion right from the start.

3. **It seals the deal.** There's just something about cutting out those photos, the ones you've built a whole life around at this point, that seals your belief that this will one day be your reality. Each time you look at those pictures, the movie in your head begins to play. The vision of the day they come to life begins to feel real—that's their magic.

4. **It is continuous motivation.** When you have a physical board on your wall (mine are in my bedroom and at my desk), they are in your aura all day, every day. Those pictures evoke your subconscious vision whether you spend time looking at the board each day or not. Just having them around you stimulates your dreams, belief, hustle, vision, and hopes for the future. All of that works together to keep you motivated and focused on the life you are building, even on the most frustrating days.

Whenever I'm questioning my dreams, or trying to get over a tough setback, all I need to do is look at my #FutureBoards. Spending just a few minutes playing the internal movies associated with each picture is enough to rekindle the fire of desire and motivation in me to keep hustling for my dreams.

A Step-by-Step Guide to Assembling Your #FutureBoard

It's finally time to make that #FutureBoard! Here are the steps you need to follow:

Step 1: Buy a Beautiful Cork Board

These days it's pretty easy to find a stylish cork board. They are normally in the office section of most big-box stores, but sometimes you can also find them in the framed art section. Get one that matches the artistic vibe of the room you want to put it in. If you can't find what you're looking for in those stores, there are always a few plainer options at office supply stores. You might also try a craft store. It's important that the board looks beautiful hanging on your wall; you want it to add to the decor. Mine are like large pieces of framed artwork.

Step 2: Print Your Pictures

Now that you've created your online Master #FutureBoard it should be full of photos from each of the five categories. The easiest way to print these photos is to open each picture up, one by one, and paste it into a blank Word document. You'll notice you can drag the image to make it larger or smaller within the Word page. I'd suggest not making them any smaller than half the page. You want them big enough to show up on your board.

When your Word document is full of all your photos you can then print it at home if you have a color printer (and fresh ink or toner). If you don't, just save the document and email it to yourself or save it to a USB drive. Head to your nearest copy or print shop and (color) print the document. It might cost a few bucks but it's worth it!

Step 3: Gather Your Supplies

You will need: your board, your printed photos, clear tape, scissors, a glue stick, and maybe some push pins or straight pins (depending on what material your board is made from).

Step 4: Set the Vibe

Now that you have your board on hand, it's super important to set the right vibe. You want to have an optimistic, happy mindset throughout this process. Ideally you'll feel hopeful and a little excited.

Light some candles. Pour some wine. Put on your favorite playlist. Set up all your supplies in a comfortable place, maybe on the carpet or a large table. Take a quiet moment before you start to sit in meditative reflection. Close your eyes and repeat mottos similar to the following:

- I am open and ready to receive the life I am creating.

- I am worthy of this new, abundant life.

- I am grateful for all I've been given, and thankful for all that will begin manifesting from today forward.

- I will receive the gifts of this new life with grace and a humble, grateful heart.

- I will bless others when I am blessed.

- With greater abundance I will positively impact more people's lives.

- I will be open to new opportunities as they arise and be patient in the journey.

- I am excited for my future.

- I am eagerly awaiting what the Universe has *already* put in motion on my behalf.

- I have joy.

- I am happy and grateful.

- I am abundant.

- I am successful.

- I am living an AMAZING LIFE!

The more you repeat these mottos, the faster they will change your beliefs and outcomes. Print them out and put them by your bed at night. Read them out loud when you look at your board on days when you need that extra motivation.

Step 5: Assemble Your Board

Cut out your printed photos so they each look like individual pictures. They will be various sizes and shapes, which is perfect. Once they are all cut out, begin arranging them on the cork board in whatever way looks best to you. I always find that somehow they magically seem to fit together perfectly like a puzzle. So play with the arrangement for a bit before pining, taping, or gluing them down to ensure it's the look you want.

You don't have to put the photos on the board in categories; they can be randomly placed. However, I normally do put my "career" photos together, and the other categories together, just so I can see the clear picture of my future life in each section. But that is just my own little thing, it's not a requirement.

Step 6: Hang It Up!

This is the most satisfying step of all! Get a hammer and a nail and mount your beautiful new life on the wall. Place it where you'll see it several times a day. In one house I lived in, my #FutureBoard was proudly displayed above the mantel in my living room.

This step might actually feel a little awkward and that's okay. I can't tell you how many clients try to get out of hanging up their board! It's crazy: they will have gone through all this work, done all the homework assignments, and then *beg* me to let them get out of hanging it up. Sorry folks, no free passes! You *must* hang it up.

You must hang it up.

The very first board I ever made was in 2007, back when I was still married to my ex-husband and pregnant with my twin girls. I'd spent the whole day making it after watching *The Oprah Winfrey Show* about "vision boards" and was pretty proud of myself. That day, when my husband came home from work I showed it to him. He looked at it, then at me. Anger and contempt flickered in his eyes. He was so upset that I'd wasted an entire day on something so "stupid" when I could have spent that time stressing about our financial situation and preparing to move because our home had just gone into foreclosure.

I was so embarrassed and ashamed that I put the board under our bed. When our home was foreclosed on and we moved into a crappy little rental house, I hid it in an old closet. It wasn't until after he left that I found the courage to finally bring it out of hiding.

Not one single thing manifested during the two years my board was in hiding. Less than a year after I displayed it (and plastered my walls at work with the photos of my new dream life), I began manifesting. It's not a coincidence.

Don't hide your dreams.

Don't hide your dreams. If you're too embarrassed or ashamed to display a photo of your dreams because they feel "ridiculous" or embarrassing, how will you ever be comfortable *living* them? The process of living them starts here.

No matter how uncomfortable it feels in the beginning, that uneasiness and embarrassment soon fades. It's not long before your board becomes part of your home and part of you. As the weeks and months pass, you'll notice your dreams no longer seem as crazy or unrealistic. In fact, each time you glance at your board, excitement begins to replace doubt and fear. The magic has begun!

You'll notice a deeper motivation replacing old feelings of uncertainty. Now you *know* what you're working toward; your life has direction. You catch yourself gazing at it one day and it comes alive in your mind. Now each photo has a specific day, a future memory, associated with it. You feel hope and excitement for the future and gratitude for how far you've come.

By the time your board is one year old, you'll be utterly convinced that one day you will live those dreams. You will want them more than ever before. Maybe you'll have already lived a few. It creates in you an undeniable transformation, and it's a magical way to live!

One of the other questions I'm often asked is "How often do I make a new board and what do I do with the pictures from my old board?"

When I first began manifesting I didn't really know what I was doing or how this all worked. So I kept my first board up until about 70 percent of it had manifested, which was about two years after I first displayed it. My motivation behind making the new board was simply because I got tired of looking at old pictures of moments I'd already lived!

That started my personal tradition of putting all the old photos that I'd already manifested in a special box in my closet. I love pulling that box out at the beginning of a new year and adding all the new manifestations from the previous year's board. Most of the time the pictures are a bit faded and worn from being on my wall all year, but that just makes them extra special.

I want dreams that scare me, but also give me excited butterflies.

Then I print and frame the photographs of my kids and me *living* those manifested moments. They create a beautiful photo gallery covering the entire wall of my staircase at home. It's a wall that's forever growing and expanding, as more and more once-in-a-lifetime moments continue to manifest. It's my favorite place in our home. I call this my "reality wall." Every photo on that wall is a moment, a memory from my *real life*, that started as a dream on my #FutureBoard.

So what do I do with the old photos that didn't manifest yet? Those are a great place to push the boundaries of my dreams. Because I've been surrounded by them for a year, they no longer seem so unattainable. They no longer scare me. I want dreams that scare me, but also give me excited butterflies.

So I ask myself, "What's the next level to this dream? How can I push myself to make it bigger?" For example: If my "old" picture was of a woman flying first class, the bigger version of that dream might be to fly on a private jet. So that's a photo I'd look for until I found the perfect one, and then I'd use it on my new board.

Occasionally I'll remove a photo from my old board when the dream it represents is no longer relevant. It happens, we change. Our dreams change and grow with us and that's a good thing. It doesn't mean we "failed" because we didn't get to check that one off the list; it means that we are paying attention to our heart and adapting our journey accordingly. That's a good thing.

I now create a new #FutureBoard every year, on January 1. It has all new photos. It represents bigger versions of older dreams, but it also displays brand-new dreams. Each year I do all the homework you've done in this book. I ask myself those same tough questions, because I never want to just float through my life. Each year I want to push myself, to reexamine what I want and make sure it's still in alignment with what makes me happy.

I have several #FutureBoards around my home at this point, but my master board is always the most important. It's the board that displays all five categories of my future life. Your master board should always include several photos in each of those categories as well. But it's also okay to make additional boards that expand on one or more of those categories.

For example: I have a board dedicated to travel. It's one of my core passions and I am in a state of near euphoric joy when I'm thinking of, planning for, or actually traveling, especially when my children are with me. Because travel plays such an important role in my life, I want to be surrounded by lots of pictures of those once-in-a-lifetime moments.

I also have a board dedicated to career dreams and goals that sits behind my laptop at my desk. In my bedroom I have one wall that is essentially #FutureBoard wallpaper! It's covered with seven boards showing many examples of my future life. But my master board, in the center of it all, is that exact same cork board from 2007 that started it all.

My hope for you is that the board you've just created is your first, but absolutely *not* your last! I want you to make a new one each year as well. Do your homework again next year, and the year after that. It's a journey that has no end. Just growth, manifesting, and forward progress.

Oh, and by the way, that first board I made in 2007 has now manifested every single picture, except Oprah! But fear not, my darlings, because even that is on its way! In the summer of 2018 I flew to Los Angeles where I met with Sheri Salata (former president of Harpo Productions and executive producer of *The Oprah Winfrey Show*), where I had lunch at her kitchen table while we discussed a project we are working on together involving #FutureBoards!

See? Nothing is impossible!

Summary

This chapter covered how to make your physical #FutureBoard, so I know it was an exciting one for you! How does your board look? Where is it hanging? Don't you just love it!

We also addressed many of the questions people have asked me over the years about how I make my #FutureBoards. I hope you've found those answers helpful and I hope they addressed all your questions.

If not, feel free to tweet me your question, my *Twitter* is @sarahcentrella or ask it on *Instagram* or *Facebook*.

I'd love to hear from you. I'd also LOVE to see your #FutureBoard, so post a pic of it and tag me. Also, use the #FutureBoards hashtag and I can repost it or share it in my story on *Instagram* @sarahcentrella.

PART THREE

AFTER

You've Made Your #FutureBoard, Now What?

Now that your beautiful #FutureBoard hangs proudly on your wall, the process of manifesting those dreams begins. There are several components to manifesting successfully. Think of it as a recipe, like making bread. A basic bread recipe needs flour, water, salt, and yeast, right? Skip the flour and you won't have bread; skip the yeast and your bread won't rise. Manifesting is like that.

Most people are under the impression that manifesting requires only dreaming, but that would be the equivalent to the water in the previous bread recipe; it's necessary, but definitely not the only ingredient.

This section will give you the recipe to manifesting once your board is complete. It's the piece most traditional "vision boards" lack.

In this section you'll learn:

- How to become *obsessed* with your dreams, to proactively speed up the manifesting process, helping you "see" and "feel" your dreams before they happen.

- How to turn on your *hustle*, giving you control of creating this new life. You'll see why working for your dreams is not only the key to success, but also a way to actively begin living them now.

- How to be patient while waiting for your manifestations and opportunities to arrive. You'll also learn how to trust this process, even when results don't happen on your timeline.

- You'll learn my New Year's process for updating your #FutureBoard and starting this process anew each January. I share my personal manifesting rituals, which have greatly increased the speed and accuracy with which my boards come to life.

So let's get started!

10: GET OBSESSED WITH YOUR NEW LIFE

In this chapter you will discover the important role obsession plays in speeding up the manifesting process. I understand obsession has some negative connotations, but I will teach you how to use it in a positive way, to help you "see" and "feel" your dreams before they happen. I will share how to transition your obsession from dream to dream as you begin realizing them, keeping up momentum.

Obsession is the key to self-creating relentless determination, hustle, razor focus, passion, clear vision, and excitement around your dreams and future life. It's one of those qualities that separates successful people from the masses. Let's learn how you can harness this tool to your best advantage.

Obsession Is EVERYTHING!

In all my work with professional athletes, obsession was one of those common denominators they all possessed. They didn't just want to live their dreams; they were *obsessed* with every aspect of them. Their friends were athletes and coaches. Their free time was spent practicing, working out, or studying plays. Their entire lifestyle was built around achieving their goals.

Unfortunately, obsession is often something many athletes lose upon retirement, leaving them feeling lost and ungrounded. If they're unprepared to shift focus and obsession to the next transition of life, it can be devastating.

Postpartum of a Dream

When you manifest a dream, one you've obsessed over and worked toward for a long time, an unexpected emptiness can fill the void afterward, leaving you unmotivated and possibly a bit depressed.

It's something I personally experienced after the release of my first book, *Hustle, Believe, Receive.* I'd spent an entire year obsessed with getting that book written and published; it was all-consuming. The naive part of me, who'd never previously gone through the publishing process, thought it would become an overnight success. I planned for my life to change dramatically with immediate effect. But it doesn't always work that way, does it? Manifesting doesn't follow our schedule; it happens when the timing and circumstances are optimal to support our greatest success.

Six months after my book's release, I found myself in a mild depression. *How could this be?* I kept asking myself. *What's wrong with me?*

It took me

Why am I not "Living the dream?" I'd manifested the outcome I wanted, which was to get the book published and reaching number one in its categories on *Amazon*, so why was I feeling like a failure?

a minute

to realize

I was

missing the

obsession.

It took me a minute to realize I was missing the *obsession*. Instead of being hyperfocused on a goal, the way I'd been for the previous year, I was in "wait and see" mode. I'd stopped taking action. Without consciously realizing it, I'd been waiting for something big to happen, rather than continuing my hustle and adapting my dreams.

Take it from me, it's a shitty place to be. You may have experienced something similar in your own life, after achieving a major dream. Brides can feel this way after their wedding, a sense of let-down once the festivities are over. College graduates can experience this after a lifetime spent learning, then being thrust into the "real world." Stay-at-home moms often go through it when their kids start school full-time.

It's an underlying sense of *now what?* Followed by: *Do I have the energy to start over and find my next "thing"?*

You can feel a lack of passion and purpose in your life, as though you're drifting aimlessly. This happens whenever you're not actively driving your life. Focusing solely on today is the quickest way to lose sight of, and stop guiding, your future. Complacency is a killer. It eats away your days, months, and often years, before you've reached a point where drastic change is unavoidable. For this reason, I want to teach you how to create and channel obsession to your advantage.

How to Become Obsessed about Your New Dreams

It's easy to understand how athletes can be obsessed, they probably started wanting their dream in grade school. But how does a person get obsessed about turning a "crazy idea" into a company? Or building a business? How do recent college graduates become obsessed about their future when they're likely starting at the bottom? How do you get obsessed when you're sick of your job?

The answer is the same for each scenario: obsession and passion are self-created. Even athletes didn't get obsessed overnight. It came through constantly practicing their craft, playing that sport in video games, being around fellow athletes, having posters of favorite players on their walls, watching *SportsCenter*, working with trainers, coaches, and nutritionists. It comes by spending time thinking about those dreams more than anything else. Imagining what it will feel like to play at the highest level, against athletes they've admired, in front of family and friends. They can envision what that life will look and feel like. The more they do this, the more motivated and obsessed they become.

Ways to Create Obsession

Now it's time to get creative. How can you further surround yourself with your dreams on a daily basis? Try these suggestions:

● Continue practicing the skills you learned in Part One of this book to grow your imagination skills, helping you *see* your new life.

- Each time you imagine one of your dreams, try to expand it. How can that dream become more vivid? More life-like? Continue growing it in elaborate detail.

- Talk about your dreams and the life you're building—don't keep it a secret!

- Allow thoughts of your new life to float in and out of your consciousness with greater frequency each day.

- Spend time online searching for photos and seeing different variations of your dreams.

- Read (or listen to) books about people who've lived dreams similar to yours.

- Watch movies about people living similar dreams.

- Follow people you admire on social media.

One caveat about that last point though, as it can be a slippery slope. Be careful not to follow too many leaders in your given field when you're just starting your journey. There's a real danger of getting so wrapped up in observing the success of others that it can actually be extremely *demotivating* over time. Also, you'll run the risk of being less original. Since everything you see and hear impacts your subconscious and forms thoughts, carefully protect your mind space; it's easily influenced. The worst is getting sucked into a rabbit hole and comparing their success to your beginning journey, which is an easy way to kill your flame. I've seen this cripple so many people who have amazing stories to tell, but are too intimidated to get started.

Personal Example

I've dreamed of visiting Italy since I was eighteen years old. The first seeds of which were planted in my senior year of high school. I'd driven my white 1970s VW Rabbit sixty miles to the nearest theater with my boyfriend (who later became my ex-husband) to watch the movie *Only You*, with Marisa Tomei and Robert Downey Jr. It was the first time I'd ever "seen" Italy. I was transfixed.

I'd always known my grandparents where from southern Italy; I'd taken pride in my Italian heritage my entire life, but I'd never actually seen what it looked like. Hard to believe, I know, but I was raised in a…let's just say, nonconventional way. I wasn't exposed to TV, movies, or secular books until I was fifteen, so that movie transported me to a world I'd never known.

I remember driving back home that night, telling my boyfriend that *one day, that will be me.* I'd be standing in a wooden speedboat heading down the Grand Canal in Venice. I'd drink wine from a bottle in Tuscany and get trapped driving circles through roundabouts in Rome.

When I was twenty, I planned to backpack through Italy, writing and taking pictures for a month. I researched that trip, saved the money, and then eventually chickened out. It happened again in 2013. I'd convinced myself *this was the year!* I was really gonna go. But I didn't. I let fear stop me again. Fear of not being able to afford it, of being gone for weeks, of having an ocean between me and my babies.

I'd had enough of fear and indecision!

But in 2016 something in me snapped. (This was about the time I'd recognized my lack of obsession after my book was released.) I'd had enough of fear and indecision! I was over waiting.

I made a concrete decision, one I spoke out loud to the Universe. "I am going *this* year!" I said. "*And* I'm taking my babies with me!" I knew it sounded crazy, hell, I knew it *was* crazy! But I didn't care, the time had come.

And then I got *Obsessed*.

I rewatched *Only You* with the kids for the hundredth time. I told them we would go somehow, some way. I began listening to traditional Italian music all day long. I watched every movie filmed in Italy I could get my hands on. I read books and novels set in Italy. I spent hours poring over maps and tracking the routes we'd take. I looked up train fares and schedules. I filled an Airbnb board with housing options in just about every major Italian city! I spent countless hours online finding places to go, things to do. The kids and I downloaded a language-learning app and began using our limited Italian at every opportunity.

In June of 2016, just weeks after that decision, I got an email alert that flights to Rome had been slashed by 50 percent. I stared at it, knowing full well this was the Universe's way of saying "Oh, yeah? I'm calling your bluff!" I knew I couldn't really "afford" it, but I also knew that has always been my excuse.

I also knew that manifesting comes in the form of an opportunity, one that often requires us to take action based on faith, even in the face of fear.

I closed my laptop. "If the sale is still going in three days, when I get my commission check, I'll do it!" I told myself. Those three days passed with a mix of excitement and dread. What if the sale ended? What if it didn't? If it didn't, I'd have to push past all my fears and reservations; I'd have to keep my word. Both options terrified me. I checked my email frantically several times a day. I checked and rechecked the flights.

The night before my check was due, I stayed up waiting for the direct deposit to hit my account. One screen refreshing my bank balance, the other checking the tickets in my shopping cart. At 4:00 a.m. that June morning, I clicked the purchase button. I don't think I've ever been so nervous in all my life!

What was I doing? I'd never traveled outside the US with my kids! We didn't even have passports! We didn't know the language. How would I pay for the rest of the trip? A million doubts and questions swirled, but when the ticket confirmation hit my email, they began to fade. This was *real*. We were going to Italy in just over three months! I ran into the kids' rooms shaking them awake, excitedly giving each the news.

The Universe always has your back.

Three days after buying the flights I got an unexpected client, which more than covered the flights. A month later, an old court case settled in my favor, which paid for the rest of the trip, making our Italy adventure one of the fastest manifestations I've ever experienced. My faith and action were rewarded.

The Universe always has your back.

Without even realizing it, our three weeks in Italy closely mirrored the movie *Only You*. Our first experience was getting on the private wooden water taxi, taking in the breathtaking views of Venice from the Grand Canal. We rented a tiny Fiat and drove through Tuscany, getting lost on little roads in remote hilltop villages. We got stuck in the exact same roundabout in Rome. We put our hand in the Mouth of Truth. When we returned from Italy, the kids and I watched the movie again and counted twenty-seven parallel experiences.

That's the power of obsession! These dreams implant themselves into our subconscious and can show up later without conscious planning or effort. They guide our decisions and actions from a primal place within us, one that might not connect those dots until later.

That's how obsession can turn thoughts, dreams, and images on a #FutureBoard into life-changing memories.

Act On Your Dreams

My dream of Italy alone was not enough to manifest the experience. It was twenty-three years from the time I first had this dream to the time I lived it. A photo on my #FutureBoard was also not enough (not fast enough anyway!). I first put pictures of Venice, Tuscany, and Rome on my #FutureBoards starting in 2007 and continued with new images on each subsequent board. It was nine years from the time I put the first picture of Italy on my board to the time I went.

What finally did the trick? Obsessive action! It was about three weeks from the time I decided I was going and became creatively obsessed, to the time the opportunity showed up. But *nothing* would have ever manifested if I wasn't willing to take that initial leap of faith. I *knew* it was a sign and I also knew the ball was in my court. If I didn't act it would just be one more time when I chickened out. Taking action, even in the face of doubt and fear, is what gets the ball rolling. It's you meeting the Universe halfway.

From the time of my decision to become actively obsessed to our opening memory of Venice was about four months!

homework

Grab your journal and think: What are some of your dreams? How can you find creative ways to surround yourself with them on a regular basis?

Write down five dreams. For each dream, brainstorm at least five ways to creatively surround yourself with this dream.

Hint: Think of what you watch on TV, or what you listen to. How can you incorporate your dreams into these two powerful mediums? The things you see and hear play a huge part in influencing your subconscious mind. Could you choose podcasts or audio books that have something in common with your dreams? Can you meet new people who are already living similar dreams? Can you learn the language, take a class, get a mentor? Can you change your phone screensaver to a picture of one of those dreams? Can you make a new #FutureBoard dedicated to one of those dreams?

Get creative. Remember that everything you see, hear, read, speak about, write about, and are around, is *already* influencing you. So how can you tweak those things to gain the maximum benefit?

REAL-LIFE SUCCESS STORY

Madeline Roosevelt
OREGON, USA

Before I met Sarah in 2017, I was a single mom of three. I felt depressed and lost, so much so that I sometimes felt like ending my life, because I couldn't find a way to provide for my children. Life was difficult. I wished for a support system, anyone I could count on or turn to for emotional or financial support, because I didn't have that.

After working with Sarah and learning her methods for manifesting, I made my first #Future-Board. On it, I put pictures of everything I wanted my new life to become. Such as photos of a happy family and the experiences I wanted to have with my children.

I dreamed of one day getting married again, and went so far as to write a letter to my future husband, describing in great detail the man I wanted to marry. But most importantly I wanted to buy a house so my children would have a safe and secure home.

Once my board was complete I began working on changing my mindset, from one of depression based on what I didn't have, to one of thankfulness every day for what I did have. Sometimes it was gratitude for something very small, because it seemed like there was nothing big to celebrate. I learned to be grateful for the crappy car I had at the time, thankful that it took me from point A to point B. I became grateful for the room I had at my parents' house, because I was not homeless, even if it made me feel less confident than living on my own. *At least I have a roof over my head*, I reminded myself every time I wanted to complain.

In 2018 I met and married the love of my life! I even manifested the dream wedding and a honeymoon to Italy! In 2018 I also manifested my ultimate dream when I was able to buy a home for my family, set beautifully on 9.6 acres!

This method has delivered more than I could have ever imagined! Now I truly believe that *anything* is possible for myself and my family.

Obsessive Action

Obsessive action is the difference between wishing for something and making it happen. You have so much more control over your outcomes than you realize. Sitting around waiting for your dreams to beat down your door is *not* a strategy! It doesn't work. You've got to recognize opportunities when they come and have the courage to take action. That courage comes from wanting your dreams more than your excuses. Wanting it so bad that you're okay with risk being a part of the equation.

Summary

In this chapter you learned the importance of obsession and how to create it. You also learned what can happen when you don't know how to self-create and transition your obsession to the next dream once one has been realized. And you listed ways you can incorporate these tips into your daily life, to surround yourself with your dreams, creating your own manifesting obsessions.

11: TIME TO HUSTLE!

This is the part many people dread. I know what you're thinking, and yes, you DO have to put in some work! I told you from the start, this is no ordinary "vision board" book! There's no supernatural code to punch that parks a free Mercedes in your driveway, or makes money rain, or turns unicorns into house pets! Nope, this is the real deal. It's the no bullshit truth of how to create a vision for your life, make a board to reflect it, then use both to fuel your hustle and allow the Universe to throw in a little manifesting magic to make it all come together.

This chapter will teach you not only *how* to hustle, but how to enjoy it as an immediate way to begin living your dreams. It is all about learning to take proactive action toward creating the life you want, which sets the manifesting wheels in motion. You'll also learn how to use your hustle to fuel your determination and vision. Plus, I'll show you what my hustle looks like, to give you an idea of the action I take on a daily basis to make my dreams come true.

I think this chapter is such an important key in the process, and one most theories on manifesting ignore. It's the part that gives you control over your future, which honestly feels so empowering! I want to teach you how to use the hustle to your advantage instead of dreading it. So let's begin!

Make Things Change

Manifesting is a recipe, not a single ingredient. What happens if you try to make bread without flour? You wouldn't get bread that's for sure! Hustle is the flour. "Universal magic" is the yeast. But so many people think manifesting is only yeast! They think if they wish hard enough, they'll be the one person able to make bread with only yeast. Hate to burst the bubble, but it doesn't work that way, my friends.

But don't despair because now you have the components to this recipe (the contents of this book) and all you need to do is put this recipe into action to create manifesting magic the way I have. And like making bread, the more times you try, the better you'll get at putting the ingredients together and getting the results you want. Personally, I get great comfort from this understanding because first, I know the recipe has been tried and tested and it has *never* failed me, and second, because I know it's all within my control. It's up to me, not some mysterious power I have to wait around for. If I apply the recipe, I get results. If I *choose* not to (yes I said *choose*, because from now on if you don't make the changes you've started here, that will be a choice), momentum stalls and results stop.

You play the lead role in your life.

You play the lead role in your life. Whether it feels that way right now or not, you write and direct the script of your life. Don't wait another day for things to change; make them change. Only you can make that happen. Take action, do the homework, translate what you've learned into your real life, see opportunities when they appear, and take risks—the Universe will reward those efforts.

Oh, by the way, your hustle has already begun. That's the exciting news. Each time you choose to think about your new life or your dreams over obsessing about your current circumstances, that's *hustle*. Each time you catch yourself about to start bitchin' and decide to be grateful instead, that's *hustle*. Everything you've done so far has assembled and mixed the ingredients, enabling that spicy manifesting "magic" to happen.

How to Self-Create Hustle

Not everyone is born a hustler, just like not everyone is born a "positive person." But the good news is, like everything else we've discussed, you can teach yourself *how to hustle*.

Hustling is the ability to figure it out. If you've got hustle, you're not waiting for permission from anyone, you're just charging ahead figuring it out as you go. Hustlers don't need to be micromanaged (in fact they probably hate being told what to do!). They have an ability to teach themselves skills most people would never attempt without proper training. They are like worker ants; put an obstacle in front of them and they'll find a way around it. A hustler is scrappy and will try anything if they think it will work. They are much less afraid of failing than they are of not trying. They take pride in effort and in getting the job done.

If you've got hustle, you also have confidence. That doesn't mean you don't doubt yourself or experience fear, it just means you've proven yourself, *to yourself*. You believe in your ability to get it done!

As a lifelong hustler, I've taken great personal pride in these qualities. I knew I'd never be the smartest girl in the room, probably not the prettiest, definitely not the skinniest or most educated, but I've always known that my hustle and ability to adapt to any situation means I can hang with the best of them, *regardless*. As a result, I'm not easily intimidated. Your hustle is the one thing in your life that you can always count on and control.

I get that not everyone knows how to hustle, that's okay. Dreamers, you tend to struggle with this part because it's not the big thrilling outcome you so desperately want.

Dreamers can get frustrated easily and tend to be members of the "I want it now" club. *Patience and work?* Ummm, not normally your jam.

That's why this section is especially important for you to digest.

Maybe read through it a few times, because I need you to *know* that this new life does *not* happen without your active participation. Remember that baby steps are perfectly normal, but consistency is king. So keep at it with determination.

Tip 1: Be Willing to Start from Scratch

Many people make the mistake of having big dreams without the humility and grit to start those dreams from scratch. They feel entitled to *be there already*! They've put in some work, a few weeks, maybe even a few months, before frustration sets in. "Nothing's happening!" they complain.

But what they don't realize is the people they admire, who are already living similar dreams, have actually been busting their ass for a long time. It all looks so easy from the outside, but peel back the layers behind anyone's success and you'll see how long their consistent dedication was present before results began to show. It's been said that it takes ten years of hard work before "success" materializes. There's no magic potion to drink and be there already.

When I started this career path, I knew that if I wanted to be a best-selling author, I had to first torture myself writing a book (or books). I understood that to be a top motivational speaker, I needed to book my schedule with as many speaking events as possible, even if I wasn't confident in my ability. There's no other way to become the best without getting on stages and perfecting my craft.

I got that becoming a well-known, highly paid life coach takes years of building clientele and testimonials. So I coached people for years *for free*. I wanted to become an effective coach and I needed practice. I wanted undeniable proof that my coaching method worked. Only then did I begin charging for my coaching services. Today I charge the same amount for one hour of coaching as I did for eight weeks when I started. But that was earned over time.

I was willing to put in that work for years. I started at the very bottom in each category of my current career. I realized it was just part of the deal. If my dreams are HUGE (and they are) and I'm starting at square one (which I was), then I understood I needed to hustle like crazy to create something out of nothing.

The same is true for my speaking career. My dream to become a motivational speaker began in 2011, the first time I ever put a photo of a microphone on my #FutureBoard. And God, did I suck in the beginning! I remember booking my first few speeches (unpaid of course) and writing out, word for word, what I'd say. There was no teleprompter, just me behind a podium, reading out loud. I quickly realized that wasn't gonna cut it. A few years later when I got a paid gig, I opted for a more "professional presentation" style. Halfway through it, people got up and walked out.

I needed to hustle like crazy to create something out of nothing.

I was *that bad*.

I went home afterward and cried for days. I was leveled. Why had I chosen a dream where I totally *sucked*? Shouldn't it come naturally? "I'm never doing that again," I told myself. I was so embarrassed and knew I'd humiliated the person who'd given me the opportunity.

It took me two years to get back on a stage and share my story again. This time I didn't write a speech. I didn't prepare a "presentation." I got up in front of three hundred employees at Nike World Headquarters and just told them my story, sharing the tools I'd used to change my life. I cried. Many of them cried. I laughed; they laughed. Not one person walked out.

From that day on, I've learned how to be myself on stage. To not transform into a "motivational speaker" but to be Sarah.

Now speaking to a room full of people, eager to learn how to change their life and manifest their dreams—there's absolutely no place I'd rather be! I *love* making people laugh. I love watching them have breakthroughs. Each time I get on stage I feel more comfortable and I continue to improve.

That is the hustle. It's being willing to work hard for what you love, even if you've "failed." It's also a willingness to work your way up the ladder. I spoke for free until 2017. I volunteered my time because I wanted to be *good* before I took a client's money. Because of that, when I made speaking the cornerstone of my business, I could confidently charge a premium.

Tip 2: It's Okay to Not Know It All

The other mistake newbies often make is allowing the fear of "not knowing enough" to paralyze them. Specifically, worrying they might not be adequately prepared or qualified to take action. But here's the thing: it's okay if you don't know it all! It's totally *normal*. Nobody knew it all before they began. In fact, it's the ability to move forward *regardless* that separates the winners from bystanders. Embrace it, own it. Be comfortable reminding yourself (and anyone who questions you) that you're learning as you go.

The part that matters most is just *starting*. Take that first step to make something happen. Who cares if you mess up? News flash, you WILL mess up. But every single thing you try and every action you take—whether perfect or flawed—is getting you closer than you were yesterday. And truthfully, that is what matters. That's the action the Universe

You Thinkers hate this, I know! Taking action without vetting every possible outcome? *Am I nuts?!*

But remind yourself that there's a time and place for everything, and the time for overanalyzing and over-thinking is *not* the moment when you should be taking action.

Take that leap of faith and just START.

Do the first thing on your list that will commit you to fol-lowing through on your dreams, and *then* you can do some more research. That's when you bring in mentors, coaches, or get advice from people you admire.

If you're noticing that vetting options, creating multi-ple strategies, and doing research is making you less excited about your dreams, that's a clear sign it's time to shut off your thinking cap and just start taking action. And guess what? If you stumble a few times, act impul-sively once in a while, make mistakes, or even (gasp) "fail," remember those scars are worn by everyone who's ever lived their dreams. It doesn't make you a "failure," it means you've joined the boss club!

is waiting to see, before it will begin helping you out by opening doors and bringing you opportunities.

Flawed action is better than no action.

There is no such thing as "knowing enough" before you get started. To think so is a rabbit hole that will create fear, doubt, negative obsessions, and stress. Avoid this trap at all costs by simply taking the first step and granting yourself grace. Come to terms with the fact that this will be a learning process and with each lesson you'll improve and get better. Be okay with that *now*—it will make the process so much smoother.

Tip 3: It's Not Supposed to Be "Easy"

There's this horrible rumor that says *if something is "hard," then it's probably not the right path.* This myth would make people believe that they must wait to find the "thing" that comes "naturally." But that thing doesn't exist!

Do you think a talented violinist whose dream is to play with the New York Philharmonic wakes up and says, "It's my dream, I'm talented, so I never have to practice!" People can't even comprehend how much work goes into playing at that level. It's not easy I can promise you that! Does that mean the musician wasn't talented because they had to work so hard? Of course not! So why then do we think our dreams must just "flow"? Or that manifesting them must be "easy"? It doesn't make sense!

Whether it is a dancer, actor, artist, athlete, doctor, lawyer, musician, literally *any* profession—it takes work and time to become any good!

Understanding this will help you see that you are not the only one who works hard for their dreams. In our society of "*Instagram*-perfect" lives, it's easy to convince yourself that it comes easy for others, but hard for you. But that's just a front! It's hard work for them too.

I think this knowledge really helped me not give up when obstacles came throughout my own journey. I knew that it wasn't supposed to feel "perfect" or "easy," and that gave me resilience. It kept me from questioning my path because I wasn't waiting for it to just magically "flow." I knew it was up to me to make it happen, even if it was hard.

Tip 4: Fear Is Normal and Not Always a Bad Thing

Does the vision you've created for your new life scare the crap out of you? I sure hope so! If it doesn't then you didn't push yourself hard enough in all the previous homework exercises.

Fear is normal! It's a good thing. It means you've pushed your boundaries and blown up your comfy box. It means you're making decisions and actions that are new, which is scary. It means you're moving in a direction where the outcomes are unknown because the path is also new; *that's amazing!*

Banish this myth: "If it's right for you, it shouldn't be scary." That's another nasty rumor. Scary is good! It helps you look at a situation from various angles. It forces you to weigh the pros and cons. If you can take action toward what you want in spite of fear, then you are on the right path! That is the true measure of greatness.

All those people out there living dreams you admire, they've all been scared shitless too. But the reason they are *living* their dreams and so many others aren't is because they took action *regardless.*

Tips for Thinkers

Okay Thinkers, be careful here because this is where you can really overthink things and freak yourself out!

If you find that instead of fear helping you vet your plan, it's talking you out of your plan, take a step back. Stop vetting, stop thinking about it all together for a day or two.

Focus on another part of your plan/dreams that doesn't scare you, the part that makes you happy.

Then you'll be able to come back to this in a few days with a clear head and move forward rather than allowing fear to prevent action.

Also remind yourself that this fear you're experiencing is normal. It doesn't mean you're doing anything "wrong." Ask yourself, "How bad do I want it?" If the ultimate outcome is worth the risk of whatever you're afraid of, then close your eyes and jump! Trust that this process and the Universe are not going to let you face-plant.

Have courage in the face of fear. Allow your fear to help you further vet your plan. Let it make you even more determined to succeed. Stare it down and promise yourself that you will defeat it every time.

Fear challenges you most at the convergence of ecstasy and failure. The moment right before your dreams come true is when fear threatens to take it all away. In that instant you have a choice: do it anyway, or go back with your tail between your legs. This is the intersection where success or failure is decided.

A few years ago, my best friend, Courtney, decided to go on a flying trapeze for her birthday, inviting me and a few other close friends. Now, I don't love heights. I actually didn't even realize how much I dislike them until the exact moment I stood below the two-story trapeze contraption and watched my friend and all the other girls take their turns, yelping with glee. I knew my time was coming; I mean, you can only skip a turn so much before everyone realizes what you're up to.

Finally, there was no one left but me. I climbed the shaky ladder, with each step allowing fear to take a firmer grip on my psyche. By the time I reached the platform, I was in a full panic-attack mode. The rational part of my brain knew I'd go through with it—there was no way I'd be the only coward in the group! But the irrational part was fully consumed with terror! It kept screaming, "You're insane! We're gonna die!"

In that split second as the harnesses were strapped to my body I knew I had a choice. Move forward, regardless of near-crippling fear strangling my entire body, or turn around with my tail between my legs and be the one who couldn't hang (literally!). Everyone who'd gone before me yelled up encouragement. "You will love it!" they promised.

A moment later the decision was made and I was flying through the air, two stories above the nets, *alive*! I wasn't dead! It hadn't killed me after all. As I soared through the air, suddenly the fear was replaced with unexpected and overwhelming joy. I was *flying*!

Don't let fear keep you from flying.

That's how fear works. It works the same for a physical activity like that or for creating your dream life. It comes right at the moment when everything is about to come together, when ecstasy is waiting. It will always be a choice, even when it doesn't feel that way. It will be a choice if you turn around and "fail." It will be a choice if you find your courage and disregard fear to make it to the other side.

Don't let fear keep you from flying.

Tip 5: Take Daily Action

Many people simply don't know what to do to get started. That's because we often think that all our actions need to be big, bold moves. But in reality, the hustle is made up of consistent, smaller daily actions.

One question I always ask my clients to get them creatively thinking about *what to do*, is to simply make a list of brainstorming ideas. I call this my Hustle List and it's sorta like a to-do list. It's a list of things I can do today, tomorrow, and this week that will get me one step closer to my dreams.

Here's an example: If your dream is to be a top-rated podcaster and you're starting from complete scratch, what would you need to do in order to make that a reality? You might not know the answer right off the bat, so finding those answers will be part of what goes on your Hustle List.

home**work**

Pick one of your dreams for your new life and start listing out at least twenty things you can do to make it happen, like I do in the upcoming podcast example. For instance, if your dream is to travel with your family, start thinking about what you'd need to do in order to make that happen. Get passports? Research places? Find photos so you can get a clearer vision? And so on. Same goes for any and all of your dreams—use this same process. Just ask yourself, "What can I do, starting today, to make this happen?" Break the dream up into small, manageable "to do" items on this list.

Tips for Dreamers

So for you Dreamers, the Hustle List will be exciting for like thirty seconds! Because as you start writing it out, you'll be fired up to go find the answers to these questions and get your dreams started. But about halfway down the list you will sigh and read through it in despair.

You'll be like, "Oh, my God! I can't do all that! It's too much. It's too hard. Everyone else is already doing it and they are way better than me. I'll never be that good, so why even bother!" See how slippery thought slopes work? They are dangerous little suckers!

Breathe. Chill. It's going to be okay.

This list is just so you have some guidance, so you know what to start working on. It doesn't all need to be done today, this week, this month, or even this year. Hopefully there's stuff on your list that will span all those time-frames. So breathe. Pick one thing on the list to begin doing today, make it the thing you do this week. Just that *one thing*. Then when you're feeling pretty good about that, pick the next thing, and so on. Refuse to allow yourself to get discouraged. Put things like this in perspective and don't allow them to overwhelm you.

Let's try it out… So just off the top of my head, I'd say you'll probably need a microphone and maybe some headphones. You'll need a podcast hosting platform. You'll need to learn how to use it. Then how to get it connected to all the streaming services like iTunes. You'll need to figure out how to market your podcast and maybe get a website or a blog to accompany it. And so on… It's that simple.

You need to see what it will take (even if it's just a guess) to take an idea and make it real, and there's no better way than just making a simple list. It's a starting point. It's not the holy grail; it's just how you get started and stay on track. It's how you take control of your dreams.

Tip 6: Keep Hustling When It Feels Like Nothing's Happening

I get this question a lot: *How can you keep hustling when it doesn't seem to be working? When it feels like nothing is happening?*

The short answer is: *a 1 percent chance is better than zero.* If you're putting in effort on any aspect of this new life, you are upping your percentage rate. The moment you stop and accept defeat, you lower your chances of success. I'm no rocket scientist, but it seems to me that doing something is better than nothing. Regardless of how frustrating it can sometimes be. I mean, what's the alternative? Sitting on your couch eating pints of ice cream? Umm, no.

Does it get annoying when results don't appear instantly or when expected? Hell yes it does! But they *will come.* I promise, as long as you don't quit, the outcomes you seek will show up.

Pro tip: If what you've been trying really isn't working, just tweak it a bit. Once you've removed the option to give up, it's just a matter of adjusting your process. Try something new. Think creatively. Be a worker ant and find a way around it. Give the old hustle a rest for a bit, then come back with fresh eyes and a new angle. Sometimes that's all it takes to break through to the other side.

Tip 7: Be All In

You've got to make a decision, a concrete choice, to be all in. Many people wait around for confirmation from the Universe, but that's not how this works. The decision is yours; it's up to you. Are you going to be 100 percent in on this new life? On your dreams?

Until you make that decision, you won't ever see real progress or success. And that's what everyone's waiting on, right? "Well, if I can just start seeing enough success, then I'll know this is the right path for me." It doesn't work that way, friends. The Universe is waiting for you to make that call on your own, because it's the people who choose to be all in *regardless* who reach their goals and live their dreams. However, that doesn't necessarily mean you make rash decisions immediately.

There are two degrees to "all in." The first is *mental* and the second is *physical.*

Let's say your dream is to start a business, but you currently work a nine-to-five job. You are "mentally all in" when you *decide* that you *will* start that business, no matter what. Period, end of story. This step removes the option to "fail" because you've committed to achieving a successful outcome, therefore regardless of what the interim process brings, you will not quit. You can be "mentally all in" while still working your nine-to-five job. It's called the *double hustle*! And boy do I know it intimately. If you're doing the double hustle you are working on your business basically every minute you're not at your "real job."

It's the perfect time to do your research, set up the business structure, build the platform and foundation, test out your ideas and products, basically get as much done as possible before you transition out of your day job and into your business full-time.

A mistake I see people often make is committing to the mental and physical "all in" at the same time, before the first part has been fleshed out. This just adds unneeded pressure and stress that brings negative energy to your new endeavor, and that's the last thing you want. The double hustle can be an amazing opportunity to work out all the kinks, while still getting a regular paycheck.

Eventually the time will come when you'll also need to be "physically all in." That's the point where you realize you've maxed out your double hustle and your two worlds are starting to collide. It can happen in various ways. You might be getting too busy with your passion project, causing you to start slipping at the real job. Or maybe the passion business has reached a point where it needs your full attention. You'll know when you've reached this second decision-making stage; it's something you've been planning for and knew was coming. It's the point where you take the big risk, leave your "real job" and become 200 percent committed to your business.

That stage will eventually force itself if you don't make the decision, and you might not enjoy the Universe's attempt at a "nudge." It's often the murky area where people wait for success to come before taking that leap of faith, but it's not going to happen. It's never going to feel like a "sure thing." It will still feel risky and scary; the Universe is waiting for you to be fully committed before those results can be seen.

Here's a perfect example. I started coaching my methods back in 2010, first on my blog, then working with professional athletes, and finally coaching individuals and groups. For seven years I built my brand and my social media platform, got valuable coaching experience, wrote a book, defined my unique method, and learned how to build a (very unique) business from scratch.

I knew it was time to transition away from my double hustle into doing my business full-time, but I was scared and dragged my feet. After all, I was still a single mom with four people to support on my own—how could I walk away from a comfortable salary to zero guaranteed income? It seemed insane. But I knew, with every fiber of my being, that my business was also my calling—it could not be ignored. I also knew I wasn't ever going to reach the levels of success I envisioned until I was physically "all in." My divided attentions were no longer serving me, my business, or my employers.

The promises I made to myself that day fortified my resolve.

So in a way, I wasn't totally shocked when, out of the blue, my employer let me go. I knew the Universe was throwing me out of the nest as it were. It was time. I remember driving home that day, repeating these words over and over again: "I will never work for anyone again. I will never go back. This is my time. It is done."

That first year was rough. I'm not going to sugarcoat it: it sucked. I'd never tried to fully rely on my business to support my family before; it was a massive and uncomfortable transition. But I knew it was necessary, it was time. Those words rang loudly in my ear each time I thought about maybe going back to corporate. The promises I made to myself that day fortified my resolve.

This all comes back to your clear vision and #FutureBoard; it's what got me through that first year. It is the foundation for everything. Manifesting opens doors for you and brings opportunities you wouldn't receive if you hadn't made your #FutureBoard, but it's not a magic wand. No one is ever an "overnight success." It may seem that way on the outside, but trust me, there's likely been years of work behind the scenes, when no one was watching. Hustle paves the way for the stars to align when the time is right.

I truly believe the hustle is what solidifies your dreams. It's the actions you take that turn a hypothetical dream into tangible reality. It's the act of *living* your dreams beginning on day one.

Tip 8: Know What You're Working Toward

What keeps me going when the journey gets a bit treacherous and overwhelming? A clear vision of my ultimate dream and the life I'm creating. I *know* what I'm working toward. All I need to do is spend a few minutes in front of my #FutureBoard re-creating the movies in my head about each picture, and I'm put right again. If I ever doubt my dreams, that board is a reminder of the life I'm building, one my old corporate life could *never* touch. My #FutureBoard displays what the payoff will be as long as I never give up. It keeps me from quitting. It fuels my hustle and relentless pursuit.

Personal Example

I was born to hustle. It's my autopilot setting. If I'm not busting my butt doing fifty things simultaneously, I'm bored, and boredom is not a good look for me. The minute I slow my hustle, the balls I've cautiously been juggling come crashing down. That's quickly followed by a sense of vulnerability. Then before I know it, I'm feeling overwhelmed and just wanna binge Netflix and drink wine!

Tips for Dreamers

The key for you Dreamers is to break down your goals and hustle into small, manageable little bites. You need to know what to work on and be able to pat yourself on the back when you've accomplished it.

Remind yourself that all these "small" efforts are making a collective big impact, even if you're not seeing instant results.

BE PATIENT.

It's like a leaky faucet. Put a bucket under that thing and it drips one tiny drop of water at a time, but before you know it, the bucket is full! Work on the small while always keeping your eye on the larger end goal.

Okay, so maybe this isn't the healthiest or most efficient process in the world, but it's just how I operate. At this point in my life, I know my strengths and weaknesses, and I understand the onus is on me to avoid opportunities for self-sabotage. As a result, I'm constantly charging forward at full steam; on multiple work-related projects, creating and growing a business, making time for my health and passions, all while ensuring my role as a full-time mom of three is the ultimate priority.

People often ask me *what's my daily life like?* Or *what's my hustle?* This is what my life looks like on a daily basis. I share this because there's a misconception that "if it's what you're meant to be doing it should come easy." That living your dream is nothing but big shiny glorious moments. And it's true, those manifesting moments will rock your world unlike anything you've ever experienced, but "real life" weaves its way through the glory and the grind.

I've always found it encouraging to know a successful person's hustle; it helps me remember that I'm not alone. And if your hustle is manic as well, you're not alone!

I also share this because I know a lot of people who don't hustle. They're the ones writing me for free advice, then never implementing anything they learn. They're waiting for some mysterious magic wand to fix everything for them. Not surprisingly, I don't know any successful people with that mentality or work ethic.

I also share my hustle here because I meet many people who tell me they don't have enough time or money to work on their dreams. To those excuses, I give you a glimpse into my life at this present moment in time...

My Hustle: It Ain't Glamorous!

As I write this, it's nine days until Christmas. But the kids and I will be celebrating early this year, on December 22, since it's the alternating year when they spend the holiday with their father. This means it's my year to be alone on Christmas, something I deeply dread.

But since it's something that is out of my control, I've got to focus on completing the preparation for our holiday in the next three days. Presents to buy and wrap, stockings to hang, cookies to bake, "Christmas dinner" to prep, and outfits for everyone to wear to *The Nutcracker* ballet this weekend.

However, all of that is proving trickier than usual because Kanen had knee surgery two days ago and can't be left unattended. The doctors repaired his ACL after he tore it playing football in the final playoff game of his sophomore season. He's fifteen years old. His dream is to play in the NFL. *Poor kid.* Thank God he's a trouper. He's one of those amazing humans born with a positive attitude. Now all his focus is directed at rehabbing quickly, so he'll be ready for spring ball. This kid has goals and dreams and he's not about to let a bashed-up knee, or a broken finger, broken ankle, or concussion stop him. Yes, he's suffered all those injuries the past few years and this is just another setback. He is facing it like a champ. He's been applying everything I believe (and teach in this book) to go from not playing his freshman year (due to injury), to earning a starting spot on the varsity team at his school his sophomore year.

It's me who's struggling to adapt. There's good news though! While I'm helping him recover, I'm spending every spare moment writing this book (just for you!) because my deadline is fast approaching.

This is pretty representative of my average daily hustle:

- Up at 6:30 a.m. to get my kids ready and out the door to school.

- Signing and shipping books and workbooks daily. Yup, I'm standing in line at the post office during the Christmas shipping rush.

- Squeezing in coaching calls wherever possible.

- Planning my New Year's Mastermind event, which is thirty days away.

- Creating content for my new online course, which is thirty-six days away.

- Planning my annual women's empowerment dinner, which is four months away, but has several upcoming deadlines. I still need a venue, sponsors, gift bags, volunteers to help day of, photographers, videographers, to book the guest speaker's travel, and get contracts out.

- Figuring out how to use the new webinar tool I've just invested in so I can conduct my first live webinar next week.

- Finalizing my retreat schedule and content for the upcoming year.

- Sending speaking and workshop quotes.

- Trying to stay current on my social media posts and email blasts.

- Updating my website (constantly).

- Working with partners on joint projects, each with individual looming deadlines.

- Unpacking my suitcase from last weekend's speaking event in Palm Springs.

- Packing my suitcase for my solo trip to Paris over Christmas.

- Cooking dinner with my girls, because it's Sunday and we always cook Sunday dinner together.

- Taking Kanen to physical therapy.

- Responding (whenever possible) to countless messages and online comments.

- Finding someone to stay with Kanen for ninety minutes tomorrow, so I can get in a hot yoga class.

- All the normal mom stuff: laundry, constant housecleaning, grocery shopping…you know the drill.

- Meditation and journal writing before bed.

- When I'm finally in bed each night (around 1:00 a.m.) I listen to Audible until I fall asleep. It's probably a novel or memoir about a woman living in Italy. Because one day I'll live there and I need my dreams to be reinforced while I sleep.

Unsurprisingly, my goal for the coming year is to build a team and delegate! At the moment I (attempt to) manage all of that on my own. No nanny. No chefs. No house cleaners or assistants. No social media people. This is *my* hustle. But I know (with confidence) it won't be this way forever. That knowledge keeps me going. One day I will have assistants, managers, marketing and PR people, financial people, full-time employees, house cleaners, chefs, drivers, and personal trainers! I'm willing to work this hard now because I know in the end the rewards will be well worth it.

Like I said, living your dreams isn't all glamorous moments; it's hard work people! It can be grueling and often thankless. There are frequent setbacks and disappointments along the way. Big deals fall through, doors close, opportunities don't pan out, people let you down. I'm not special or immune; I go through it just like everyone else.

But even on the most challenging days, I'd NEVER, EVER, trade this life for *anything*. Not for the security of a six-figure corporate salary, not even for full benefits and a retirement plan! This life is worth the pain of a broken marriage and the struggle of starting from nothing. It is so worth it.

And your dreams are worth it too. Living them will be worth all the sacrifice, hard work, heartaches, setbacks, struggle, and everything you've endured to make them a reality.

Summary

We covered a lot in this chapter because it's such an important part of the manifesting process. Your homework—creating the Hustle List—showed you that there are things big and small you can do on a daily basis to get closer to your dreams.

As a reminder, these are the eight tips for self-creating hustle:

1. Be willing to start from scratch.

2. It's okay to not know it all.

3. It's not supposed to be "easy."

4. Fear is normal, and not always a bad thing.

5. Take daily action.

6. Keep hustling when it feels like nothing's happening.

7. Be "all in" on your new life.

8. Know what you're working toward.

REAL-LIFE SUCCESS STORY

Stephanie Thavixay
WASHINGTON, USA

"I learned just how much the Universe always provides and rewards our belief."

In 2015 I made my first #FutureBoard while participating in Sarah's group coaching program (an amazing experience by the way)! At the time I was in full hustle mode, trying to get my business off the ground. I actually connected with Sarah because she featured my story in her book *Hustle, Believe, Receive*. I had the hustle part down, but was missing the other key pieces to manifesting the life I wanted until going through Sarah's program.

On that first board, I put places I wanted to visit and things I wanted to do, such as New York City, California, and a family road trip. I also put photos of a brand-new car, a new home, some equipment for a small business that I wanted to grow, a small boutique where I could sell my clothes, and photos that represented emotions like happiness and joy.

Without even fully realizing it, I'd manifested everything that was on my first board! It's crazy, because so many of my original dreams from my #FutureBoard became my reality while I was in the thick of hustling.

Sometimes you forget, or don't realize, that everything you're working toward now all started with the dreams you put on that board.

In January of 2016, when Sarah's book was released, I scraped together every penny I had to make it to New York City for the red-carpet book launch. Less than one month later, Sarah invited me back to New York to participate in an ABC News event for the book and I remember being so afraid because I didn't know if I'd even have enough money to eat on the trip. But I knew it was an amazing opportunity for myself and my company, so I took a leap of faith and went. As it turned out, I learned just how much the Universe always provides and rewards our belief. I wound up getting bumped from my return flight and offered a $1,000 American Express card by the airline as compensation! So I actually made over $600 for making that trip and trusting the process!

A year later I was making a stable income with my business and able to buy myself a brand-new 2016 (right off the lot) mom van!

Now my kids can ride in comfort and Mom is riding in style! A year after I purchased my car we went on a family road trip to California.

At the end of 2017 I found a business partner with an equal hustle and together we opened a print shop for my business in early 2018. When we started, it seemed impossible. But our vision was clear, and we knew what we wanted to create, so we made it possible. We rolled up our sleeves and turned the place into a storefront where we can sell and display my clothing line and print client orders in the back.

In 2018 I was able to quit my nine-to-five "day job" and take on running my business full-time, which is a dream come true. Five years after starting my business, selling T-shirts on a blanket in the park, I am now a bona fide entrepreneur!

In the fall of 2018 my parents sold our childhood home. We searched high and low for a new place to live, and at the absolute last minute as the papers were closing on the sale we found the perfect home, big enough to fit my whole family.

We went from an old moldy house to a spacious new beautiful home. Even though letting go of my childhood home was bittersweet, I am beyond grateful to live with my parents and help them with their needs, while my own family has a beautiful roof over our heads.

Everything I originally dreamed of has manifested, though not all exactly in the way I thought or expected it would. I've realized that I don't control the timing, and that things can happen in ways you would never expect, and that living this life has brought me so much joy and happiness on a day-to-day basis.

It's also taught me that everything ALWAYS works out, and that stressing about how it will turn out is a waste of time—it's better to spend that energy on your hustle!

Now it's time to make a new #FutureBoard!

12: BE FLEXIBLE AND PATIENT

It's hard to be patient, I get it. I might be the least patient person I've ever met! I am the queen of "I want it NOW!" But I've learned how to relax (a bit) and allow this process time to work. This chapter will teach you how to be patient during the journey, so you won't allow frustration to cloud your judgment or cause you to question your dreams. It will also teach you how to recognize when your manifestations are showing up as opportunities from sources and directions you'd never have expected.

It Takes Time

All good things take time to grow. You might think you're as ready right now as you could ever be, but patience is preparing you. There must be another lesson, or another person you're supposed to meet, or more practicing of your craft that is needed, because there is always a reason for Universal timing.

It's easy to question yourself, the process, God, the Universe, everything, when it seems like "nothing is happening." But don't stress, you're not doing anything wrong, you haven't messed up the method: *it just takes time.*

Whatever you are going through right now, you are experiencing the *exact* education, process, experiences, lessons, "failures," losses, wins, that you *need* in order to become successful and live your dreams.

I know it's hard to hear, but you need to be right where you are. Whatever you're going through, no matter how shitty it seems, trust that it's all needed preparation, getting you ready for the next level of your journey.

Learn the Lessons

Are you paying attention and uncovering the lesson you're meant to be learning in this "downtime"? Are you making the most of it? Are you asking yourself every day, "What should I be learning from this process so that I never have to repeat this experience or relearn this lesson?" That is your goal in the quiet times between big wins. Be smart, learn the lesson the first time so that you can move forward, grow, and never repeat this experience.

I know it's hard to remain patient when it feels like *nothing is happening*; trust me, I know. But believe me when I say (from exhaustive experience and repetitive lessons) that your dreams *are* happening, the process is working even when you can't see the results.

Think of it like an oak tree. It doesn't sprout from a seed overnight into a giant shade tree. It begins by digging its roots into the ground, setting a foundation that will hold the weight of the tree as it grows. That's what's happening behind the scenes when you're hustling, believing, envisioning, daydreaming, and changing your mindset—all of that is planting roots. Some results show quickly, others take a while, but *all* of it is working.

Use This Time to Prepare

So many people waste their energy throwing tantrums because what they've tried for two weeks hasn't delivered yet. Don't get caught in that trap; instead focus on how you can be more prepared and better prepared for the moment your dreams come to life. What can you do today that will make you better?

I think of the very first book I wrote in 2012. Back then I thought it was ready for publishing and was devastated when that dream didn't materialize. But looking back now? Oh, God, I am soooooo happy that book never got published! And I'm not at all surprised it didn't. It sucked! I was a terrible, inexperienced writer. I'm no Hemingway now either, but I am happy that it took several more tries (and a *lot* more practice) before one of my books was ready for publishing. So use this time to your advantage. Get prepared.

How to Keep the Faith

It is hard to keep faith in your dreams when it seems like nothing is happening, but try these tips to keep yourself on the right path:

Recognize and Shut Down Doubt

Doubt is so dangerous. Unchecked it will spread like wildfire destroying all the positive work you've done. Doubt surfaces when you've stopped focusing on your vision for the future or when you've stopped hustling. Here's a rule to check yourself: if you're hustlin' and focused on what you're creating, you ain't got time for doubt!

Keep your mind busy and focused on what you want, on gratitude, on where you're going, and why you want it. When doubt starts saying things like "You know, this isn't working, maybe everyone was right, maybe you can't do this." Or "If this was meant to be, it would be working by now." Or "Who do you think you are? How are *you* qualified to live this dream?" Or whatever your negative voices are trying to convince you of, you must immediately shut them down!

Recognize it as the voice of doubt and realize that its job is to try and sabotage your success. That's a thought that does *not* serve you! So respond with: "Not today! You are *not* going to get me down and make me start doubting everything. Not happening!"

Tell Yourself the Outcome You Want

If your dream is being tested, it's because you've stopped focusing on your future life and the outcomes you want and started thinking about your current circumstances. You've transitioned from a place of excited gratitude and hope for the future to a "poor me" mindset. It can happen in the blink of an eye. It can sneak up on you from out of the blue. But the more you learn to recognize the signs, and understand those thoughts lead you down the wrong road, the quicker you can self-correct. Constantly tell yourself that the outcome you want is coming, it's happening.

Stop accepting negative thoughts as fact. Create a new story by saying things like:

- I can do this! I was born to do this!

- Things might be moving slower than I'd like, but that's only temporary.

- I *know* I'm on the right path and in the right place.

- I am learning more every day.

- Every day I am getting closer to my dream and am more prepared for my moment.

- My moment *will* come. It is already on its way!

- I cannot wait for that moment when I am *living* my dream!

Daydream

Immediately begin daydreaming about what that moment will feel like. Who will be there with you? What will you be wearing? Where will it be? How will you feel? How will you look? What photos will you take to mark the occasion that will one day hang on your wall? Remember: Don't entertain doubt. Entertain hope.

It's Happening, Even When It Seems Like Nothing's Happening

Here's the awesome news, guys! While you're resisting the urge to beat your head against a wall because it seems like *nothing's happening*, the Universe has been busting its butt behind the scenes to line everything up for your big manifesting moment. And when that happens, it can seem like everything just magically fell into place overnight! It's the most intoxicating feeling. It's like waking up lucky one morning and everything you touch turns to gold!

But here's the thing: it was in process that whole time! That's why you can't lose faith in the "slow" times, and that's definitely why you can't give up! Just keep pushing forward. Eventually the floodgates will open, and everything you've been dreaming, hustling, and praying for will happen in rapid succession.

Manifesting Will Come As an Opportunity

Your manifestation will come in the form of an opportunity. And it will probably happen when you least expect it. Because it's all been working behind the scenes, manifesting will often happen in a way you could have never imagined—sometimes from a source you'd have never expected. That is why it's so important to be ready, and recognize the opportunity when it comes. In my experience, manifesting is almost always disguised as an opportunity. Because of this you need to be aware and ready to take action. Believe me, you don't want to miss your big opportunity like I almost did.

Personal Example

The year 2017 was one of those years where it seemed like all hustle and no results. It was rough. I was questioning everything. It was my first year walking away from my corporate job and transitioning to the life of an entrepreneur and it wasn't pretty.

I remember just begging the Universe for a sign. "Just give me a sign that I'm not insane!" I begged. "Drop me a crumb!" Have you ever been there? Where you're just like, *dammit, give me one break, just one!* I was there. It was December 2017, I was stressed. I'm not going to lie, I was really wondering if I had what it took to start and run a business.

One day, in the midst of my fist-shaking and tantrum-throwing pity party, I got an email. It was from a podcaster named Ed Mylett. He asked if he could interview me for his show—he said he'd read my book and loved it. I remember reading his message and pouting. *What will one more podcast interview do to help this situation?* I asked myself and closed my email.

A week or two passed and I was still choosing to remain in my funk. Yes, I knew it was a choice. I didn't care. I knew how to get out of it, but I didn't want to. I realized I'd stopped hustling and focusing on my dreams, which was why I'd landed in said funk. But I just didn't have the energy to shake it. I wanted to go on feeling sorry for myself.

Then another email came from Ed, asking again if he could interview me for his show. *What can it hurt?* I thought. This time I responded. Immediately my email buzzed; it was Ed. "Can you call me right now?" he asked. *What the heck!?* I thought, so I called. "I just have seven minutes, but I wanted to connect with you quickly," he said. "I loved your book!"

homework

Grab your journal whenever you are going through one of these downtimes and answer these questions to try and help you positively navigate it.

- What could I be doing each day that will get me better prepared for when my moment arrives? What is this trying time teaching me?

- What lessons should I be learning right now?

- How can I perfect my craft so it's ready for the big moment?

- What thoughts have I been thinking the last month? Am I self-creating a "funk"?

- How can I refocus on my dreams and my future life in a way that will bring me renewed joy and focus, helping this time pass more quickly?

He had my attention!

I remember hanging up the phone and thinking, *that seven-minute conversation just changed my life*. I didn't know how, but I just knew it. I pulled up his *Instagram* (@edmylett, you should totally follow him, he's amazing!) and the last video he posted was one where he talked about how your life can change in a day. "You never know who you'll meet, or how it will happen, but your life can change in a single day." I knew instantly that message was for me. It was the Universe trying to shake me from my funk. Trying to beat me over the head so I wouldn't give up and miss my opportunity.

That seven-minute conversation just changed my life.

All the time I'd been hustling "without results" it had been lining everything up for me to succeed. Luckily I'd spent 2017 getting ready for a moment like this, and in February 2018 when our podcast interview aired, my life changed in a day.

The day the interview went live, my book (which by that time had been out for two years) went from unranked to the top 100 on *Amazon* in a matter of hours! That month I booked speaking gigs totaling more than I'd made the entire previous year!

Don't do what I did. Don't willingly choose a funk and nearly miss your big moment. Be ready and stay ready, because it's coming! And when it does, it will probably be in a way, and from a source, that you never saw coming.

Summary

In this chapter you learned how to spend your "downtime" when it seems like results are taking forever. You learned how to use this time to prepare for your future and learn the lessons this time is meant to teach you. You learned how to keep the faith by:

- Recognizing and shutting down doubt.

- Telling yourself the outcomes you *want*.

- Using daydreams as a tool to refocus your mind.

You were also reminded that even when it feels like nothing's happening, the process is still at work. And because of this, when it does happen, it can seem like an overnight success. And most importantly, manifesting happens in the form of an opportunity, so be ready! Stay actively focused and don't discount any opportunity because you never know which is the one that will change your life.

REAL-LIFE SUCCESS STORY

Belen Flemming
MINNESOTA, USA

"My manifesting momentum has been unbelievable!"

I learned about Sarah's manifesting method through reading her book *Hustle, Believe, Receive* in 2017. When I realized she was coming to Minneapolis for a #FutureBoard workshop, I purchased the VIP ticket that included a one-hour phone coaching call with Sarah prior to the event. She brought existential clarity to my life during our conversation because she knew how to understand highly sensitive people like myself. I got off that phone call feeling truly validated for the first time in thirty-nine years.

Sarah encouraged me to broaden the scope of my life and gave me permission to take my dreams to new heights through showing me how to dream HUGE and seize opportunities. Over the years before meeting Sarah, I'd manifested big dreams including a second chance at a beautiful nuclear "family life," going from being a single mom with one child to having a partner and a new baby. I had been extremely focused on manifesting a second child and it happened! But just weeks before I spoke to Sarah, my reality of a beautiful family of four collapsed when my partner decided to leave the relationship.

Sarah helped me realize that I'd been so focused on visualizing adding a baby to my family that it was what had manifested and not necessarily the lasting relationship. I hadn't taken the time to imagine how the life I wanted would *feel* when it manifested.

Leading up to Sarah's #FutureBoard workshop, I dove into completing all the homework and learned how to create my online #FutureBoard in her class. Since then, my manifesting momentum has been unbelievable!

During Sarah's workshop I wrote down what I wanted in my future life; it was hard and uncomfortable to write down dreams I'd never put on paper before. Then I wrote down the big "pipe dream" using two powerful words: "I am." I wrote: "I am a published photographer." Two years ago I had left my corporate marketing job to follow my dreams and start my photography business, but I'd never before stated that I wanted to become a published photographer.

The next morning I awoke to an email from an editor of a local print magazine saying that he was hoping to include a story about my photography business in an upcoming issue! Four months later, I received a text from a neighbor telling me

she'd just read the article about my photography! Two weeks after receiving that first email my work was also published online in a premier design publication, *Domino* magazine.

A few months after Sarah's workshop I attended a panel discussion called *Finding Your Voice in Reinvention*, featuring author Laura Munson. Her talk focused on her own reinvention and brought to mind my #FutureBoard and desire to expand my dreams in new directions. A few weeks later I received details about a writing retreat she was hosting in the mountains of Montana. I had put a photo of a mountain-themed office on my #FutureBoard, and took that as a sign to attend her retreat. I sent Laura a photo of Sarah's book with the caption "Sarah told me I need to think broader!" To which she replied, "Open up the book and go to the index. And you will find one more sign."

So many things have manifested from my #FutureBoard, both big and small. It's already been an incredible journey and it's only been a few months! Imagine what a few years can do?!

Laura Munson's story was featured in my book Hustle, Believe, Receive!

13: MY NEW YEAR'S MANIFESTING RITUAL

New Year's Eve and New Year's Day traditions are a bit different in my home. It's an almost sacred time to redo all my homework, reflect on the previous year, record the "wins," and dissect the lessons from the "losses." It's when I redo my #FutureBoard and write my intentions, mottos, and goals for the coming year. It's also when I take responsibility for any negativity I might be harboring and release it, bringing only positive energy into the new year.

It's such a powerful ritual that I wanted to share it with you here, in hopes you'll adapt it for yourself. I've done versions of this at different times in the past ten years, but on December 31, 2017, was the first time I did them all together on New Year's Eve, and the results were astonishing!

Because your dreams evolve over time it's important that your #FutureBoard, goals, plans, and hustle all reflect those changes, so you never find yourself drifting or complacent. Having this annual ritual ensures you'll continue guiding your future and creating the life you want.

Note: I think it's totally fine to also do this ritual around the time you make your first #FutureBoard as well. So if you've done your board (and I know you have, *right?*), add this ritual now as your final homework assignment. Another great time to do it is when there's a new moon or supermoon. Both of these bring amazing manifesting energy to this process.

The Birth of a New Tradition

In December of 2017 my childhood friend Lisa was visiting from New York City for the holidays. She is like-minded and has been practicing these same techniques with me for the past few years. So when I told her I wanted to start a new tradition and manifesting ritual for the New Year, she was down! We grabbed our journals, some little antique bottles with cork stoppers, and matches, and drove the seventy-eight miles to the Oregon Coast.

We began our ritual by writing a letter to the Universe, containing all the deepest desires of our heart. We each wrote it in silence, pausing occasionally to stare at the stunning Pacific Ocean. The winter sun warmed our faces as we took time to reflect in meditative silence. I wrote and wrote, page after page, spilling my heart to the Universe. I didn't want to miss a thing! I told it everything I wanted, every desire of my heart and why I wanted it. Once our letters were complete we sealed them in our beautiful little antique bottles.

Then we took out our notepads and wrote our goals, #LiveList, affirmations, mottos, and plans for 2018. We took our time, meditating between each one. Taking in the beauty around us.

Our final step was to write down all our negative beliefs, feelings, and thoughts that have held us back. This is where we listed any of our blocks to manifesting and remaining beliefs that have sabotaged our success and kept us from reaching our full potential. I'm normally not a fan of writing anything that's negative, because the act of writing a thought gives it so much power, but for this exercise it is very important. It helps you acknowledge the belief, see it on paper, and detach from it.

We wrote these using a specific format: "I release the old belief that I was...not worthy of success." Or whatever the belief was. Because words are so important, we made sure to put them in past tense and add the words *I release* before stating the negative belief.

Then we burned those pages. As the flames engulfed our negative beliefs we verbally set them free and stated our new positive affirmations. These affirmations were the opposite of our negative beliefs, and we said them aloud, claiming them, as the pages burned. There was such peace watching those words—fears, doubts, negativity, beliefs, and struggles—burn. It was as if the Universe was figuratively and literally absorbing them as they turned to ash, mixing with rock and sand. The energy shift we both felt was intense! We were *free*!

We'd set our dreams free, given them over to the Universe!

Finally, we took our little bottles with our letters to the Universe, climbed the massive sea-crusted rocks, and threw them into the ocean. We were both filled with such a sense of immediate joy and release! We'd set our dreams free, given them over to the Universe! We'd made a plan and a promise to do our hustle and work every day to reach these dreams. We released all the thoughts that have held us back. It was perhaps the most empowered, cleansed, and at peace I've ever felt.

As we left the beach, the full moon began to rise as the sun set beyond the horizon. I've been going to this beach for over twenty years and I've *never* seen a sunset and moonrise like that...it was magical.

As I said, the results have been mind-blowing!

The next morning, on January 1, 2018, I put the following photos on my #FutureBoard. They are followed here by the details of how those dreams came to life in 2018! And these are just the pictures on my board! I have many more that have manifested from my *Pinterest* boards, and I reached most of the financial and business goals I'd written down that day as well.

- **London.** In May, my kids and I visited London for six days.

- **An office.** In April I got an office in the nicest area of downtown Portland, one that looked oddly just like my photo!

- **A new home.** In June the kids and I finally moved from a tiny place we'd lived in for five years to a beautiful new home.

- **A rose-faced diamond-encrusted Rolex watch.** In June I got a rose-faced diamond watch (though not a Rolex) for my birthday!

- **A photo of two girlfriends meditating on a beach.** This is how the year started with my girlfriend Lisa and me meditating on the beach.

- **Friends eating together at a dinner table** (at the time I was living in a very small space and didn't have space to entertain or host dinners). This year I hosted Thanksgiving dinner for the first time in eight years in our new home.

- **Photos of writing and books** (indicating I wanted to write *this book*). In October I signed the book deal that led to your holding this book in your hands right now!

- **Several photos of women speaking on stages.** This year I did on average two keynote speeches each month!

- **A black Mercedes.** In June I got a black Mercedes!

- **A kitchen with dark hardwood floors.** Our new home has dark hardwood in the kitchen!

- **Photos of a woman doing yoga and getting in shape.** In October I decided to try the keto diet and lost ten pounds. I also started doing hot yoga and began feeling physically great for the first time in a while!

- **Train in Scotland.** In May the kids and I rode the train from London through Scotland.

- **Horseback riding.** In July the girls and I went horseback riding in Bend, Oregon. It was the first time I'd been on a horse since I was fifteen years old.

- **A cottage in the countryside.** In May we stayed at an adorable cottage in the middle of a field (just like the photo) in Ireland.

- **A table of women eating dinner together and having a great time.** In May I hosted a women's empowerment dinner in Portland, where seventy women came for dinner, drinks, inspiration, and connection!

- **A beautiful white master bedroom with blush-pink accents.** My new bedroom is all white with blush-pink accents and a wall full of #FutureBoards!

- **A laptop on a table in Paris** (indicating writing in Paris).

- **A woman in Belgium, deliriously happy.**

And Lisa? Her deepest wish was to manifest the love of her life, something she'd wanted for many years. She also wanted a career that was fulfilling, flexible, and fed her passions. In May of 2018 she met the love of her life and they now live together in Manhattan. In June she found the job/career path she'd been seeking and now does what she loves for a living!

As I finish writing this book, I do so from a café in Paris. I have come to Paris, alone for Christmas, a dream ten years in the making. I've come to write, to reflect on all that's transpired, to refill my soul with gratitude, and to recharge my batteries with travel.

It's one of the dreams I'd written in my letter to the Universe, and it's a photo that's been on every #FutureBoard the past ten years. It's surreal to be living this enormous dream—to pause every so often and gaze up at the Eiffel Tower in front of me! Part of me can't get my head around it. Can't process it. I am here. This is real!

I'd give anything to bottle this feeling and give it to you. I want you to know what it feels like to drink champagne while looking at the Eiffel Tower, or eat a Belgian waffle at a Christmas market in Belgium, while the ancient church bells ring out Christmas carols (as I did on this trip). It's a feeling unlike anything. It's joy that wraps your body in fuzzy warmth. It's a smile you couldn't dim, even if you wanted to. It's a sense of wonder, gratitude, and love for life that nothing else has ever touched. Manifesting moments like these are what I live for!

This is how I can give you that feeling, that joy. I can share my secrets for how to do it. I can give you countless examples of how it works. I can provide the work I've done to make it happen. I can give you my recipe. This book is all those things; it's your gateway into this incredible life.

My wish for you is a lifetime of moments just like this.

Share them with me, will you? I'd love to hear your stories!

And now it's time for me to sign off, because it's New Year's Eve and I have some homework and rituals to do! Hmmm, what should I put on my 2019 #FutureBoard?

Index